Wintergreen

Wintergreen
SUPPRESSED MURDERS

Anna Elisabeth Rosmus

translated from the German by Imogen von Tannenberg

University of South Carolina Press

Published in Columbia, South Carolina, by the
University of South Carolina Press

Manufactured in the United States of America

08 07 06 05 04   5 4 3 2 1

Library of Congress Cataloging-in-Publication Data

Rosmus, Anna.
[Wintergrün. English]
Wintergreen : suppressed murders / Anna Elisabeth Rosmus; translated from
the German by Imogen von Tannenberg.
  p. cm.
  ISBN 1-57003-509-1 (cloth : alk. paper)
  1. Passau (Germany)—History. 2. Passau (Germany : Landkreis)—History.
  3. World War, 1939–1945—Prisoners and prisons, German. 4. World War,
  1939–1945—Atrocities. 5. Holocaust, Jewish (1939–1945)—Germany—
  Passau (Landkreis) 6. Prisoners of war—Germany—Passau (Landkreis)—
  History—20th century. I. Tannenberg, Imogen von. II. Title.
  DD901.P3R5513 2004
  940.53'1853355—dc22   2004014584

Publication of *Wintergreen* was made possible in part by a grant from the Samuel
Tenenbaum Fund.

For all the innocent victims of Passau's many notorious
National Socialists and their equally guilty collaborators

CONTENTS

ILLUSTRATIONS

FOREWORD

The subject of Anna Rosmus's research is the history of her hometown, the city of Passau, and its neighboring communities. Yet she is not a regional historian in the conventional sense; her writings deal with much more than just Passau society. With admirable temerity, she has dedicated herself since her schooldays to exposing and unveiling iniquities, in many cases concealed and suppressed to this day, that were committed under the National Socialist reign of terror. For this work she has been honored around the world—while in Passau she is ostracized as someone who has brought shame upon her own home, who has, as the locals say, "dirtied her own nest." And so this book, with its charmingly idyllic title, *Wintergreen*, is anything but pleasant reading for many of her compatriots. The title of *Wintergreen* was chosen with a sense of bitter irony, as the wintergreen plant was the cheapest means those in charge of keeping up the grave sites by orders of the Allied forces had of maintaining the graves of countless victims—prisoners of war and "workers of alien descent."

This is an important book, a necessary book, a book that will break taboos as it breaks the silence, that will shake us out of our stupor, that struggles against selective amnesia. *Wintergreen* deals with the forgotten concentration camps and concentration subcamps and the horrific crimes committed there: the suppressed murders of Jewish and Eastern European forced laborers and their newborn, or yet unborn, children. Anna Rosmus documents, in an effort unprecedented in Germany and in a manner guaranteed not to leave readers cold, the abortions of healthy children carried out at the Hutthurm hospital. Yet these murders have never been atoned for and would likely have never been revealed had it not been for the "unhealthy" inquisitiveness of this young regional historian.

The reality of slave labor, which was part of everyday life in Germany during the war, whether in the wartime industries or simply out in the fields, has been met with utter silence during the decades following the war. All the more infuriating is the fact that Anna Rosmus once again had to battle long and hard against local authorities and the local diocese of the Catholic Church to gain access to the files and the evidence of these crimes during her research of this book.

Based on the documents she was able to dig up, Anna Rosmus reconstructs the cases of the mass murder of Russian POWs committed in the Passau area during the final hours of the war. This, too, has been kept silent until now. Obviously the perpetrators of then are still able to exert their influence today. In several cases there seems to be no willingness for atonement, remorse, or insight. From this reluctance it is only a small step to denying the fact that these horrific crimes were ever committed—which should give us particular cause for worry in these days. For such would mean that the few surviving victims, rather than being compensated for what they endured, are violated once again! Passau is just one of the countless places where similar actions took place. The thesis posited by Alexander and Margarete Mitscherlich, of the nation's inability to mourn, sadly seems confirmed here.

In addition to these troubling facts, *Wintergreen* documents the history of the Jewish postwar community in Pocking-Waldstadt, the site of the former Pocking concentration camp, which was reconstituted as a displaced persons camp for Jewish survivors. This story contains striking parallels to what is happening throughout Germany today. The local population, led by its former mayor, found the idea that Jews would once again be living among them as free individuals hard to swallow, and so they viewed their new neighbors with suspicion and resentment. Soon barracks housing Jewish refugees began to mysteriously catch fire; once the last Jews had finally vacated the camp in 1949, there was an unconcealed sense of joy. When plans for the accommodation of a new group of refugees were made known, this time of German origin from the Eastern territories, two thousand citizens rose up in protest against the fact that "foreigners again" would be living there. In the end the camp area was dedicated to a different purpose.

In *Wintergreen* we read about these events with a sense of dread. Those who do not learn from history are doomed to repeat it. Young people must learn that social egotism, xenophobia, and right-wing extremism will inevitably lead to catastrophe. Books such as this one ought to be part of every curriculum.

Ignatz Bubis, former president of the
Central Council of Jews in Germany

ACKNOWLEDGMENTS

The publication of this book would not have been possible without the generous assistance of many individuals, administrative authorities, and institutions and without their desire to discover the truth. In particular I would like to express my gratitude to the following: the late Lucjan Dobrosycki, former director of YIVO institute for Jewish Research in New York City, for the unlimited access to all archival and photographic material; Yad Vashem in Jerusalem, for granting me access to photographic material; Staatsarchiv Landshut, for the uncomplicated access to essential and, until now, unpublished documents; the U.S. Department of Justice, for extensive support during my research, and particularly Bob Waite, senior historian in the Office for Special Investigation; Professor Barbara Ceranowicz in Warsaw, for contacting former slave laborers; Dr. Radu Joanid, director of the photo research department, and Genya Markon at the U.S. Holocaust Memorial Museum, Washington, D.C., for granting free access to the photographs; Pnina Spetgang, former director of the Holocaust Remembrance Committee, Toronto, for making possible contact with and the search for survivors of the Holocaust; the late Rabbi Lipot Yehuda Meisels and his family in Jerusalem, for granting access to photographs and documents; Miriam Griever in Dallas, Texas, for much information and for giving me access to documents; Beth Hatefutsoth, at the Museum of the Diaspora, in Tel Aviv, for granting access to photographs; the Museum of Jewish Heritage, New York City, for its kind support; the late Dr. Robert Kesting of the U.S. Holocaust Memorial Museum in Washington, D.C., for his most helpful support in searching for documents; the late Sydney Schachtmeister in Houston, Texas, for information and making possible contact with survivors of the Holocaust; Abraham Eiboszyc, and all the other survivors, for their honest interviews where no subject was taboo; Ulrich Zimmermann, the former editor in chief of the *Passauer Neue Presse*, for allowing me to use the newspaper's archives; the district attorney's office of Passau; the Berlin Document Center; Max Mannheimer and Karl Schulsky, for their translations from the Yiddish; Herr Fengler and Herr Schaffner from Passau, for granting me access to documents; Shelly Shapiro, director of Holocaust Survivors and Friends in Pursuit of Justice in Albany, New York, for her tireless efforts in establishing contacts and organizing events; Rabbi Paul Silton in Albany, New York, for making possible the close contact with Jews and Jewish organizations; the city administrations of Plattling and Gangkofen, for their kind cooperation; my uncle, Dr. Walter Friedberger, for convincing the priests of Hutthurm, Ruhstorf, and Reicheneibach to grant me access to the death registers; the many eyewitnesses, for their patience and their availability in answering unpleasant questions, thereby making it possible to gain insight into the horrors of the past; Oberstleutnant Wunder for providing the site map of the Pocking concentration camp; Max Moosbauer Jr., for granting permission to inspect and ultimately publish the de-Nazification documents of his grandfather; the Verwaltung Bayerischer Gärten, Schlösser, und Seen, the military archive in Freiburg im Breisgau, and the Zentrale Stelle der Landesjustizverwaltungen in Ludwigsburg, for granting access to explosive file material; Felix Kuballa of the WDR television station for his patience, his excellent advice, and his friendship; my family for their extensive and generous support in all situations and at all times; and Scott Evan Burgess, for his assistance with the text.

Wintergreen

CHAPTER 1

Mass Murder of the "Offspring of Alien Descent"

Between the years 1939 and 1945, close to ten million men and women from countries occupied by the German armed forces, or Wehrmacht (primarily Poland, the Soviet Union, and France), were deported to the German Reich and conscripted into forced labor. During the final years of the war female forced laborers were often assigned to work on farms. Many were sent to Lower Bavaria. In a hospital north of Passau, those who became pregnant were "persuaded" to have abortions. The children of those who managed to give birth perished in so-called children's homes.

When farmers were ordered to the front and asked to sacrifice their lives in a senseless war, replacements were needed at home. But as farm labor was grueling and poorly paid, workers were hard to come by. The Nazi regime considered various remedies, as local agriculture was at the time an essential industry and source of supplies. Initially the burden was forced on the prisoners of war. When their numbers became insufficient to fill the widening production gaps, however, girls and women from the occupied and plundered territories in the East were promised food and shelter if they would agree to sign up as "workers for the Reich."

Thousands enlisted to escape the starvation inflicted upon their homelands. Once in Nazi Germany, they received passports and work permits. When the first female forced laborers arrived in the Passau region in 1941, they were commended for their youth, their beauty, and their industriousness. "Nice girls, they were, and very respectable," some farmers still comment today. The farmers had to pay somewhere between eighty pfennigs and one reichsmark per woman daily, payable to the party, the NSDAP—a type of human rent for cheap labor. The girls were given a place to sleep and generally just enough food to be able to complete the work they were forced to do. But as the war dragged on and food became scarcer, the treatment of the so-called Eastern workers rapidly deteriorated accordingly. Thousands of women from Poland, the Ukraine, and Russia were then simply abducted and turned into slave laborers.

When inevitably some of the women, not infrequently as a result of having been raped by locals, became pregnant and fainted during work, Dr. Franz Oswald, who at the time was a doctor at the hospital in the nearby town of Gangkofen, ordered these women to return to their homelands, according to instructions he had received from the party. It is wholly conceivable that word spread among the women about this "ticket home," as there were significantly more pregnancies recorded by the year 1943. Accordingly, regulations imposed by Dr. Conti, chief medical officer of the Reich, became increasingly strict:

Pregnancy no longer disqualified women as unfit for work. Not even tuberculosis or epilepsy could get one sent home. When the children were finally born, these so-called offspring of alien descent were centrally registered and "removed," as determined by the state.

In the legal decree of 9 March 1943 (RGBl I Nr. 27), as ordered by the cabinet council of the Ministry of Defense, and as stated in paragraph 5, abortions as well as sterilization of Reichs Germans were strictly prohibited. Two days later, however, on 11 March 1943, it was revealed that Dr. Conti had made the pronouncement that the termination of the pregnancy of an Eastern worker or a Ukrainian woman would not be a punishable offense, as long as she consented to the procedure. To what degree this "consent" was actually a "forced consent" in the Passau region can no longer be definitively determined. As the decree issued by Dr. Conti was not made public until September, the German Bishops' Conference did not object until 24 September 1943. After all, the Fifth Commandment forbids the taking of innocent life. However, just one week later the Medical Association of the Reich in Berlin approved abortions being performed on Polish women as well. And so the mass murder of the "offspring of alien descent" had begun.

The Abortions in Hutthurm

Under the aegis of a medical decree issued by the district association of Passau, Dr. Franz Maria Clarenz of the hospital in Hutthurm, a small community twenty kilometers north of Passau, performed at least 220 abortions on Eastern workers between the end of 1943 and April of 1945.

Dr. Clarenz was in private practice, but he also held an official position at the Hutthurm hospital. Approximately a dozen of the abortion cases were women from his own district; all others were referred to him by the administrative region of Lower Bavaria and other districts even further away. Later, the local newspaper *Passauer Neue Presse* (*PNP*) stressed that the "legal form" had been observed and that the medical commissioner of the government of the Upper Palatinate and Lower Bavaria, Dr. Max Hartmann, had "ordered" the abortions and was himself simply following directions issued by Dr. Conti.

On 20 January 1949, the following headline appeared in the Pfarrkirchen edition of page five of the *PNP*: "THE 'MASTER OF ROTTAL' TO MAKE COURT APPEARANCE." The person referred to in this article was the Birnbach physician Dr. Max Hartmann, who represented the last "big case" for the courts. Hartmann had held numerous distinctions within the district administration of Griesbach, having served as the *Kreisleiter* (district leader), as well as *Kreisschulungsleiter* (district training leader), *Abschnittsleiter* (section leader), *Kreisbeauftragter des Rassenpolitischen Amtes* (district deputy of the office for race politics), *Gauredner* (spokesman of the Gau), *Gauobmann im Ärztebund* (Gau deputy of the medical association), *Oberführer* of the SA (supreme commander of the SA), and *Sonderbeauftragter des obersten SA Führers* (special envoy to the SA leader). In three cases, Hartmann had issued orders for "protective arrests" and had had four persons deported to a concentration camp; in other cases he was accused of using harassment and the threat of financial ruin. He not only approved the abortions at Hutthurm, but in some instances had even ordered them himself.

Hartmann was ultimately sentenced to eight years in labor camp by the Passau courts. An article published in the *PNP* on 9 February 1949, with the headline "THIS IS DR. HARTMANN," reported the following:

> Last Sunday, a citizen of Birnbach wanted to take a look at a room that had been recommended to him and his family by the local housing authority and was located in one of the two houses belonging to the Hartmann family. When he tried to explain to Dr. Hartmann that he could only come to Birnbach on Sundays since he worked out of town during the week, the landlord [Hartmann], who had recently been sentenced by the Passau Federal Court to eight years in a labor camp, showed little sympathy. Max Hartmann refused to let him see the room. It was "against all common decency to disturb him on a Sunday," he

said, adding: "I may have been indicted, but I still am Dr. Hartmann." These words were ringing though the hallway as he rudely dismissed the visitor.

Dr. Hartmann lived in Birnbach, where he remained in private practice as a general physician, until his death in the 1970s.

On 30 December 1943, Johann Winkler, the parish priest of Hutthurm, "respectfully" addressed the Episcopalian diocesan authorities in Passau. He "considered it his duty to report" that Dr. Clarenz had

> taken a child from a Polish unwed mother. The baby was dismembered while still inside its mother's womb. The mother had supposedly given her consent. Other similar cases can safely be assumed to still be taking place. Polish mothers are being brought to the local hospital from surrounding districts. A doctor has to request permission for every single procedure of this nature from the appropriate authorities in Berlin. There does not seem to be a consensus among local doctors as to whether abortions may also be performed on married mothers of Polish descent.

According to Report 164/13, number 3904 from the State Archives in Landshut, Bavaria (hereafter referred to as StAL), Winkler clearly indicated that the Sisters of Mercy employed at the hospital had "assisted" with the abortions, and that these procedures would have been "impossible" to perform without the help of other personnel. On 4 January 1944, the nun who had at that time been matron of the Hutthurm hospital, along with the Mother Superior of the Convent of the Holy Ghost in Passau, were summoned to appear for a meeting with Vicar General Dr. Riemer. The meeting took place in Passau.

On 27 January Dr. Riemer noted the following: There have thus far been three cases of Polish women and girls where "taking of the fruit of the womb" has taken place for which the matron herself administered the anesthesia and another Sister assisted in the operation. Riemer commented further: "Both were aware of the fact that they could not perform these services with a clear conscience," and he added: "During the last procedure, an assistant Sister began to sob uncontrollably and declared that she was being subjected to an impossible conflict of conscience." However, since "not a single doctor in the entire area was willing to come forward to perform this kind of operation, several more such procedures can likewise be assumed to have taken place." In the third case, Dr. Clarenz "took the Sisters' concerns into consideration and decided not to dismember the fetus, which had already reached the age of seven months, while inside of the mother, as originally intended, but instead, he decided to bring it out intact. The child lived for about half an hour and therefore it was possible to baptize it in an emergency ceremony. It was understood that even in this case, the death of the fetus was intended."

Paragraph two in Dr. Riemer's report reads as follows: "The matron of the Hutthurm hospital directed an inquiry to the main convent as soon as the first case was announced. Due to various circumstances a reply was a long time in coming, and when an answer was finally received, it was suggested that the Sisters were no longer to assist in such cases, but that the doctors should, instead, request the services of a midwife. This was to be arranged through the doctor's office." In paragraph three Riemer notes that he himself had "made it clear to the matron in no uncertain terms" that these kinds of medical procedures "were equivalent to murder," and that "the nuns must have no part in it." The matron then pointed out, according to Riemer, "that the doctor himself had stated the fact that if he were to do this to a German woman he would be sent to jail immediately, but that, in the case of Polish women, he had received special orders."

"The Vicar General," Riemer said, referring to himself, "then formally pronounced an absolute and binding prohibition. The matron was instructed to declare to the doctor at the very next opportunity that the Sisters were not to assist in any further procedures of this sort due to a conflict of conscience, and that they were prepared to bear the consequences resulting from any refusal on their part." Riemer also noted: "The matron thanked me for my clear directives in this matter and promised to follow them."

One day later, Johann Winkler personally reported to the vicar general that shortly after her return, the matron was informed by Dr. Clarenz that both she, as well as her assistant, were to prepare for the next abortion. The matron then refused, stating a conflict of conscience. Dr. Clarenz is said to have then consulted with Dr. Zagel, the district administrator of Passau, "who then contacted the district administration." As a result, the woman who was to be "treated" on 26 January was initially sent away. The district administrator admonished the matron to make her decision as to whether she would be participating in future procedures by 27 January, at 4 P.M., upon which she telephoned the headquarters of the religious order of the Holy Vincent von Paul in Munich, and on 28 January she traveled there for a verbal consultation. Dr. Riemer noted this fact in his records (Report 164/13, number 3904, StAL) and further wrote: "Another fact

5

worth mentioning is that the threat had been made that in the case of a refusal the matter would be handed over to the Gestapo," a state of events that "would have resulted in the worst possible consequences for the entire order."

On Saturday, 29 January 1944, the director of the Sisters of Mercy presented to the diocesan authorities in Passau written documentation of the legal circumstances pertaining to the cases, which she had received from Cardinal Faulhaber. It stated, among other facts, that, "On 18 October 1943, the Reichskirchenministerium [ecclesiastic ministry of the Reich] of the Bishops' Conference was able to ascertain that even though the prohibition of abortions was not immediately applicable to foreigners, there had been no known cases proving that any doctor had been forced to perform an abortion performed against his will. As a matter of fact, the Reichsgesundheitsministerium [ministry of health of the Reich] had specifically prohibited the use of undue pressure in this matter."

Cardinal Faulhaber's findings, as documented in the letter, are as follows: "Thus, the Sisters employed in the care of the sick similarly may not be subjected to undue pressure on their conscience. For the conscience of the Sisters, the same principles apply as previously expressed in cases of assistance . . . with procedures of euthanasia . . . and sterilization." Based on these guidelines it was agreed that the Sisters would help with certain preparatory procedures for such operations and that they also would take over the care of surgery patients, but that they would object to direct participation for reasons of conscience. In Report 164/13, number 3904, StAL it is stated that, "Threats such as the one that the Sisters would be relieved of their duties in the care of the sick at this or other hospitals will therefore not be taken seriously. It has to be acknowledged, however, that with the attempt to rape the conscience of the Sisters, this issue has tremendous, as-yet unresolved, repercussions for the collective morality of the German people." The matron told Dr. Riemer that she would be discussing the issue with the chief surgeon of the Hutthurm hospital, Dr. Worlitschek, as well as with the head of the Passau district administration office, in order to raise awareness about the fact that abortions were strictly prohibited by Christian ethics, and that for this reason the Sisters of Mercy would not be participating in these procedures. Two days later the matron reported to the diocesan authorities that chief surgeon Dr. Worlitschek did not care for the fact that the abortions were being performed at the Hutthurm hospital. According to Riemer's 9 February 1944 note in Report 164/13, number 3904, StAL, Dr. Clarenz, on the other hand, was initially still attempting to involve a particular Sister in assisting with the anesthesia and its supervision, but had finally relented, so that in the future the Sisters would not have to have anything to do with the process, "if indeed any further abortions were still to take place."

On page 8 of the 22 October 1949 issue of the *PNP*, it was reported that, "The diocesan authorities of Passau and the Cardinal of Munich" had "submitted a complaint addressed to the Reichsinnenministerium [ministry of the interior of the Reich] with the result that the ministry left the decision as to whether abortions were to be performed on Eastern workers to the discretion of the individual physician in charge. However, neither the Ärztlicher Bezirksverein [medical district association] nor Dr. Clarenz were ever informed about this new regulation issued by the ministry."

On 17 March 1944, Johann Winkler again wrote to the Passau diocesan authorities. "Most respectfully and most obediently" he reported that the hospital matron was complaining about "harassment." The consulting midwife who in the meantime had been brought in was unable to attend the fifteenth abortion. Because the Sisters refused to assist, Dr. Clarenz was forced to work alone. He became very enraged and rudely began to insult the Sisters. "If I only could get rid of you!" he said, calling them "bitches" and adding: "They should deal with you like they do with these Poles." Whether he was referring to the Polish children or to the general treatment of the Polish people was not clear. In Report 164/13, number 3904, StAL, Johann Winkler reported to have encouraged the women "not to take these insults" and at the very least, "to ask for a consultation with their superiors at the main convent."

Four days later Vicar General Dr. Riemer wrote to the director of the Sisters stating that, were she to deem it necessary, he would become more active in the protection of the Sisters. Initially, she took no further action. But by April the matron reported with great dismay that between three and five abortions were now taking place every day, some even as late as during the eighth month of pregnancy, when the children were already fully developed.

On 15 September 1944, Dr. Riemer noted

> According to a verbal report by the church beneficiary, Georg Reis, the number of killings of foreign children prior to their birth has increased significantly in recent months. Two or three such procedures are performed every day. For the next few days alone eighteen women . . . are

scheduled for such procedures. The chief physician is employing various methods to carry out these procedures. A Ukrainian man, who has
reportedly studied medicine . . . has now been called in as an assistant.
The clergy is under the impression that the blame for the increase of
these tragic occurrences is to be found in the local population; in particular, female farmers seem to be insisting that pregnant persons
undergo these procedures. The claim that there exists a regulation that
forces employers to make a report as soon as the pregnancy of a foreign
worker has been established, has thus far not been confirmed.

That same month Johann Winkler wrote yet another letter to the Passau
diocesan authorities:

> The murder of children at the Hutthurm hospital continues. More than
> two hundred instances have since been perpetrated. Just last week a Pol-
> ish woman who died shortly after the procedure (i.e., the abortion)
> was buried. This was the first death of its kind to happen under these
> circumstances—the coffin also contained the bodies of eight small chil-
> dren's corpses of various sizes.

Dr. Clarenz registered two hundred twenty abortions on the official lists.
To what extent this number was in reality surpassed can no longer be
determined with any certainty.

Cremated and Buried

Although it would seem that none of these children were born, either
via Cesarean or by natural means, apparently a total of twenty-one were,
in fact, baptized. The parsonage of Hutthurm lists in its death registry
twenty-one children and one adult woman from Poland. She is said to have
died due to an infection that developed during delivery. It would therefore
appear that the children were baptized in emergency ceremonies by the
church beneficiary, Herr Reis; thereafter they were allowed to starve to
death. It is not known where they were buried. It is assumed, however, that
their graves are located in the back part of the cemetery; today, this area is
completely neglected and overgrown, and so is hardly ever visited by anyone. What happened to the other one hundred ninety-nine bodies can
no longer be determined. Most likely many of them were cremated and the
rest were buried in unknown locations. No memorial to commemorate
these tragedies has ever existed at the hospital or indeed in the community
of Hutthurm, neither at the cemetery nor in any other public place. Nor
have there ever been any plans for the establishment of such a memorial.

Dr. Clarenz: "The Herod of Hutthurm"

Because the chief physician of Hutthurm, Dr. Worlitschek, had been a member of the NSDAP, he was removed from office shortly after the war. The American military government replaced him with Dr. Beckenkamp. On 4 June 1945, the church beneficiary, Herr Georg Reis, and Herr Winkler (no relation to the Hutthurm priest, Johann Winkler) filed a report against Dr. Clarenz at the Passau district administration. On the same day, the caseworker Dr. Reitberger—acting on behalf of the district administrator—sent the document, via the mayor of Passau, to the military government in Passau. The document stated that,

> In his function as physician of the Hutthurm hospital, Dr. Clarenz, who also apparently held the position as chief of propaganda in Hutthurm . . . performed abortions on foreign workers. The abortions were executed up to the eighth month of pregnancy. Our informant Georg Reis states that he had secretly baptized a large number of children whose birth was induced by force.
>
> It has been thus far determined that these are the only cases in Germany, at least to the knowledge of church authorities. In the early stages of pregnancy the embryos were simply aborted. In the advanced stages the children were allowed to be born before they were then subjected to death by starvation. The order for these procedures was issued, as far as the informant could determine, by the chief medical examiner, Dr. Conti, with the intention of exterminating Poles and Ukrainians. The chief of the Passau hospital, Dr. Niedermeier, is rumored to have objected to suggestions for similar procedures to be performed under his authority. The diocesan authorities of Passau made files available, which are currently being transcribed. No claim has apparently been filed with the district attorney's office. The Counter Intelligence Corps (CIC) was informed, due to the fear that Dr. Clarenz might attempt to dispose of the existing lists documenting all records of abortions and murders. Dr. Clarenz remains to this day a free man.

A short time later Dr. Clarenz was indicted by the American military government on the basis of formal membership in the Nazi Party and sent to an internment camp in Landsberg where he was held for two years. The *PNP* reported that Dr. Clarenz had been dubbed "The Herod of Hutthurm" by American magazines. After that, Dr. Clarenz set up a private practice in Fürstenzell, a town just south of Passau. On 24 June 1947, he applied for the position of chief surgeon at the district hospital at Hutthurm, his old stomping grounds. Dr. Clarenz then casually showed up for an interview at the offices of the district administration in order to advocate his application. In addition he intended to involve the Kreistag (district council) by submitting a petition (as recorded in Report 164/13, number 3904, StAL) of signatures proving that "his return . . . was in accordance with the wishes of the general public."

At the beginning of August 1948, Dr. Clarenz wrote that he was reassuming his medical duties in Hutthurm. He was hopeful that his former patients would return to him and claimed that he would "if necessary, and if so desired by my patients, perform surgery on them." He continued: "I have been in contact with fellow colleagues practicing in the vicinity who might issue referrals, and I am on excellent terms with them, both socially as well as professionally."

Dr. Clarenz submitted a list specifying the conditions under which he would be willing to work again. However, the priests of Hutthurm and Büchlberg (a small neighboring community) had seen to it that Dr. Braunhofer, a man with close ties to the church, was to be employed at the Hutthurm hospital. The Passau district administration, which had received the files for inspection, ended the investigation of Dr. Clarenz. The Hauptkammer (main court division) in Passau was provided with documented proof that Dr. Clarenz had been a member of the NSDAP since 1935 as well as the local propaganda leader; but on 3 August 1948, he was declared merely an accomplice to the crimes instead of a perpetrator, and fined five hundred deutschmarks for being a sympathizer. According to a report in the 22 October 1949 issue of the *PNP*, the district attorney did not appeal and the sentence became final.

The diocesan authorities, however, did not relent. Following a meeting with Dr. Riemer, the following article appeared in the *PNP* on 13 August 1948:

CONTESTED DECISION OF THE COURT OF APPEALS. STATEMENT OF THE CHURCH REGARDING ABORTIONS IN HUTTHURM: The Church has made known its vigorous objections to the decision of the court of appeals concerning abortions performed on 220 foreign workers during the war years at the Hutthurm hospital. It plans to contest the decision of the court of appeals, based on Article 5/1, not to consider the events that took place during the Nazi regime, by bringing the case against Dr. Clarenz before the Sonderministerium and the Justizministerium [Nazi ministries of justice]. It is intolerable that the occurrences in Hutthurm are being passed over in silence. This silence could easily be interpreted as acceptance, and would thus lead to confusion among the local population and cause them to assume that abortions were henceforth permissible; this assumption would seriously undermine healthy public morals. The statement issued by the Ministry of Health, which is destined to gather dust in a file somewhere and upon which the decision of the court of appeals is based, is not sufficient to prevent this danger. The Church requests this matter be submitted for public trial, either before a regular court or before a court of appeals. At the very least it must be established—notwithstanding the strict laws of the Church, which do not allow for a killing of the fetus under any circumstances—to what extent there existed serious health issues that may have necessitated the abortions, or whether in fact pressure was exerted by the party or by employers, which may have forced the women to request an abortion as otherwise they would have been threatened with deportation to a concentration camp. We further deem unacceptable the fact that a doctor who was known even by the foreign press as "The Herod of Hutthurm" should be able to once again practice at the very site of his previous dubious activities. This is the position of the Church authorities.

On 22 June 1945, at 2 P.M., Dr. Franz Clarenz was arrested by the American authorities. The reason given for his arrest was the fact that he represented a danger to the public. He was said to have conducted more than two hundred abortions on foreign workers and may possibly be guilty of war crimes. On 4 October 1945, Dr. Clarenz gave the following handwritten statement under oath:

My name is Dr. Franz Clarenz. I was born on 8 September 1909, in Kitzingen am Main, Germany. I live in Hutthurm, Bavaria, where I work as a general practitioner, obstetrician, and surgeon.

I received my medical degree from the University of Giessen, Germany, in the year 1935. From 1934 to 1938, I worked as a surgical assistant at various hospitals in Passau and Fürstenzell. From November 1938 to the middle of 1941, I worked as a general practitioner, obstetrician, and hospital physician in Hutthurm. On 25 August 1939, I was drafted by the Wehrmacht as a civilian reservist where I worked as a medical orderly; on or around 1 October 1939, I began work as an assistant physician for the reserve forces until I was discharged from the Wehrmacht in June 1941. While in service with the Wehrmacht I worked at the reserve military section of the Passau county hospital, treating officers and members of the Wehrmacht ranks. During this time it was also my responsibility to treat the civilian population and to perform surgical and obstetric operations. In June 1941, after I was discharged from the Wehrmacht, I assumed medical responsibility for the civilian population in Hutthurm. I joined the NSDAP on 1 May 1935. From June 1941 until approximately June 1945, the day of my arrest, I worked as a general practitioner in Hutthurm, specializing in surgical procedures.

I would like to mention that terminations of pregnancy in the case of German women could in fact be performed under the stipulation that a council of three doctors approved the necessity for such a procedure; for example, if the pregnancy placed the life of the mother at risk.

In the fall of 1943, however, I was informed during a medical conference in Passau that it was legally permissible to conduct abortions of Eastern workers and Polish women if they so chose. For a procedure of this kind I received on average fifty reichmarks, in some cases more, in other cases less, depending on the procedure; I was reimbursed by the Passau employment office. I have no knowledge where the money that was paid out to me by the Passau employment office originated.

At the end of 1943, I received a written notice from Dr. Hartmann, the head of the Reichsärztekammer [medical association of the Reich] of Lower Bavaria, saying that, effective immediately, I was responsible for the termination of pregnancies of Eastern workers and Polish women in the barracks for Eastern workers.

Around August 1944, the Russian physician Dr. Alexander Seliwanow and his wife Vera, who took on the duties of physician's assistant and midwife, respectively, were assigned to the barracks for Eastern workers. I have no knowledge where Dr. Seliwanow received his medical training and I have never actually seen his diploma. He was approximately twenty-eight years of age.

I oversaw approximately two hundred abortions on Eastern workers, including those I assigned to Dr. Seliwanow. I personally performed more than half of these procedures. The Russian doctor and his wife shared a single room at the location where the Eastern workers were accommodated. Dr. Seliwanow's medical services were first secured after the Russian town in which he lived was conquered by German troops. The abortions were accomplished by a kind of . . . scraping out of the fetus and the placenta from the uterus. These kinds of procedures were carried out within the first three months of pregnancy, using anesthetics such as ether, chloroform, or other intravenous medications. In those cases that simply required the insertion of a gauze strip into the vagina, no anesthesia was given. The gauze strip was left in place for six to eight hours, and expulsion of the fetus occurred about twenty-four to forty-eight hours later. The patients spent approximately six to eight days in the barracks for Eastern workers. Some of them went home on the second or third day, if they felt well enough to do so. Complications from these procedures included fever, bleeding, and in one case a patient died of an embolism. This patient died very suddenly. In most cases the anesthesia was administered by Vera Seliwanow, who is reported to have studied medicine.

I would like to add that a large number of full-term and live births took place in the barracks for Eastern workers at Hutthurm. For these obstetric services I was reimbursed according to the standard regulations by the German Health Association, which amounted to three reichsmarks per case.

This three-page declaration was written by my own hand and made without coercion on 4 October 1945, in Natternberg, at the M.V. camp at 10:45 A.M.

I swear to have told the truth and nothing but the truth, so help me God.

Dr. Franz Clarenz

On 8 November the American officer J. H. Hamlin corrected this statement and informed his office that the victims had been unknown slave laborers of Russian, Polish, and Ukrainian origin. The nature of the crimes was classified as "illegal abortion," which had been carried out between 1943 and 1945, and without the use of anesthetics. The officer went on to say that the defendant was married, with two sons and a daughter, and that at the time he was interned in Dachau as prisoner of war. The only accessible documents of proof were the CIC report and two declarations by Dr. Clarenz.

This CIC report, which was marked "confidential," also states Dr. Clarenz had admitted that the victims had been assigned to the German agricultural industry as well as to the arms sector; they were brought to him from locations throughout the administrative district of Lower Bavaria. He further admitted that on 1 January 1945, a shortage of anesthetics had led to abortions being performed without the administration of ether. Due to the extreme pain experienced by the women, additional personnel were present in the operating room in order to "forcefully" restrain the patients while he performed the abortions on them.

A separate report suggested that Dr. Clarenz was attempting to evade responsibility for this state of affairs by shifting the blame to his assistants. Dr. Clarenz also insisted that he had been acting according to orders issued by Dr. Max Hartmann of the medical association of the Reich in Birnbach. He was instructed to familiarize Dr. Seliwanow with abortion procedures; after a brief orientation period, Seliwanow was fully able to conduct these procedures by himself. Further confidential research initiated by the Americans revealed that Dr. Seliwanow was indeed Russian, that he was twenty-seven years old at the end of 1945, and that he had served in the Russian army prior to his capture by the Germans. He had studied medicine in Russia and worked as Dr. Clarenz's assistant.

Dr. Clarenz lived in a spacious building adjacent to the hospital; the abortions on foreign workers were performed in one of the rooms in this building. Dr. Seliwanow, however, was given a tiny, filthy room in a wooden barracks that was also part of the hospital. The same barracks housed up to eleven patients at a time, from the Ukraine, Poland, and Russia. They suffered from various illnesses. German patients had "taken over" the modern brick building, while pregnant foreign women had been made to sleep on straw mattresses that were covered with unhygienic felt and linen sheets. The hygienic standards were obviously of no concern at the wooden barracks—the opposite was true in the case of the hospital proper.

Dr. Seliwanow was still employed at the hospital at the end of 1945. Further research revealed that girls and women were kept for an average of six days at the barracks before being sent back to work; that Dr. Clarenz was reimbursed for the abortions by the medical association of the Reich; and that "as a result of these illegal procedures" he became a wealthy man. An article in the *PNP* from 4 September 1948, states the following: "It was not the case that Hutthurm was exclusively the site of abortions. There were just as many instances when children of Eastern workers were actually born." How many were born and whether or not any of them survived was not able to be determined, as allegedly no documents were available any longer. The patent registry in Berlin, where the documents were allegedly sent, however, informed me on 10 July 1992 that "[the documents] never arrived at our offices for safe keeping."

In July 1949, the Passau church publication the *Passauer Bistumsblatt* issued another report. In it, Dr. Riemer requested permission, "by special order of his Excellency, the Bishop of the Diocese," to publish a "declaration." The declaration, which was reprinted in the *PNP* without any editorial corrections, stated that the abortions in Hutthurm were to be counted among the most severe crimes against religion and humanity committed during the Nazi regime within the territory of the Bishopric. . . . There exists widespread horror and disgust among the people towards these murders, which by sheer account of their number could not have remained hidden. That these things ever occurred has greatly shaken the moral and legal foundations of our state.

Dr. Clarenz's argument, that he had been forced to take action "according to orders issued by the state," received the following commentary from the diocesan authorities:

It cannot be definitively determined to what extent the state may have pressured doctors in the cases of these crimes. However, in response to the Church's protests in these matters, the interior ministry of the Reich directly informed us that no force was applied to doctors to commit any actions that ran counter to their own conscience. Whatever the case may have been, the judges of the Nuremberg Trials determined that it was inadmissible for anyone to allow himself to be forced to commit clearly criminal acts against his conscience, and that crimes, even if committed by force, were to be prosecuted by the law.

It has also been confirmed that other physicians in the region declined to perform such abortions and that their decision in no way resulted in any harm to them. The declaration went on to state:

We are aware that the public sense of morality has been most painfully damaged due to the mass abortions. In our communications with the appropriate official agencies we repeatedly made clear that it has been our position from the very beginning that it was absolutely necessary to issue an official statement in this context. The statement must declare, in a legally binding manner, that these procedures represented, and continue to represent, profound crimes. Unfortunately the Supreme Court of Bavaria did not see it fit to initiate such a legal decree, due to its lack of jurisdiction in this matter.

The fact that these crimes have been virtually ignored by the state's authorities, or rather, that they were treated as though they had never taken place, represents an additional threat to the public sense of justice and further gives the impression that such procedures are no longer subject to prosecution. We hereby alert official authorities to the results of undue leniency in this matter and urgently repeat our request for them to take steps in favor of protecting both existing laws as well as the lives of the unborn.

As reported on page five of the 26 July 1947 issue of the *PNP*, Dr. Riemer, on a slightly patronizing note, encouraged the authorities "to affirm the teachings of the church" and threatened that "direct killing of the fetus will result in immediate excommunication." As reported on page eight of the 22 October 1949 issue of the *PNP*, exactly one month later "the court of appeals proceeded, according to article 52, to revoke the previous ruling, and ordered that the law suit against Dr. Clarenz be reopened." Clarenz's attorney, Dr. Hans Maul, lodged a formal protest of the decision on behalf of his client. The case against Dr. Clarenz went to trial on 19 October 1949—based on article 48 of the Befreiungs Gesetz (liberation law)—at the Munich Hauptkammer. Dr. Wilhelm Reichel from Passau, as well as the hospital's former matron and the former hospital administrator, were called as witnesses. The chief of the Passau hospital, Dr. Fritz Niedermeier served as expert witness. The former hospital pastor, church beneficiary Reis, was fined twenty deutschmarks for failing to appear at the trial. It is likely that the church administration had instructed Reis not to testify in court, as his testimony may have resulted in a closer investigation into the church's role in the abortions.

The court's findings stated that Dr. Clarenz had simply been a follower (and not an accomplice or a perpetrator); prosecution according to article 18 of the Befreiungs Gesetz was thus avoided. The costs of legal proceedings amounted to a total of 28,000 deutschmarks. The costs to be assumed by the defendant totaled 1,400 deutschmarks, a sum that would be further reduced by the court to 400 deutschmarks. The fees accrued during the proceedings of the first instance were to be assumed by the state. This set an embarrassing precedent, at least in the case of Dr. Clarenz. The court's mild sentence astonished many, as much more severe sentences had been pronounced in other similar cases.

Research Today: "There Can Be No Files for Something That Never Happened"

In recent years, regional papers from the Passau area published numerous articles in reference to the reform of article 218, known as the "abortion article." This conservative media campaign turned out to be very successful. In 1991, for example, the Passau legislature established Passau as an "abortion-free zone." When the pope decided to compare present-day abortions with the conditions in the concentration camps and the Nazi genocide, the *PNP* published an article with the following headline: "ABORTION

IS GENOCIDE." No one, however, seemed to remember the murders of the children in Hutthurm. Whatever happened there has long since been forgotten. As a result, my own inquiries into the matter were met with significant difficulties from the very beginning.

In a letter dated 20 October 1983, the former mayor of Hutthurm, Herr Baumann, informed me "that no documents that would be of use for evaluation existed in the community archives." In a telephone interview from 19 June 1983, Deputy Mayor Helga Gahbauer, claimed that "no documents existed at all." She would go on to state in a telephone interview from 12 June 1992, that, "she had never heard of such incidents of abortion." She also stated, unconvincingly, in a telephone interview from 19 June 1992, that there were no entries into either the birth or death registries of the community that would sustain such a claim.

The hospital administration in Hutthurm informed me that they were not in possession of any such documents and that in 1985 all files had been transferred to the central department of hospital records in Berlin. My research, however, would prove that those files never arrived in Berlin. In the past few decades the *PNP* and the *Passauer Bistumsblatt* repeatedly reported the resistance of the church. As reported in the 4 January 1992 issue of the *PNP*, the diocesan custodian, Franz Mader, wrote extensively on the "difficult times faced by priests during the Nazi regime," and Bishop Dr. Antonius Hofmann, on the occasion of the fiftieth anniversary of Hitler's seizure of power, honored him publicly. In 1980, Dr. Emil Janik, former editor in chief of the *Passauer Bistumsblatt*, authored a book, commissioned by the Bishop, with the title *Klerus und Klöster des Bistums im Dritten Reich* (Clerical community and cloisters during the Third Reich). There is not a single reference to the murders of children in Hutthurm to be found in the book. It is possible that the church elders knew about the role of some of the Sisters of Mercy in the murders and for this reason decided to remain silent on the subject. My personal contact with members of the clergy only served to confirm this suspicion.

Dr. Wurster from the Passau Bishopric archives admitted to having seen incriminating articles both in the "District Publication of the Passau Bishopric" (1949, number 125, pp. 48f) as well as in the *Bistumsblatt* (1949, number 14, p. 2) but he went on to present a bizarre web of evidence designed to show that the abortions never took place. He said that the fact that he can detect no indications whatsoever in the correspondence generated between the diocesan authorities and the Sisters of Mercy "for even

the slightest evidence of such abortions," led him to the "most logical conclusion in the world: namely that there can be no files for something that
never happened." Strangely enough, he sees in his conclusion a "concur-
rence with . . . the statement issued by the diocesan authority in 1949."

The fact that Walter Ziegler's book *Die Kirchliche Lage in Bayern* . . .
(The situation of the church in Bavaria . . .) "almost certainly" would have
mentioned the abortions in Hutthurm, but in fact did not do so, is considered "yet another indication that they did not take place," according to
Bishopric archivist Dr. Wurster. He finds "no such documents in the—as
yet only partially organized—estate of Bishop Simon Konrad"; also, "a
special prohibition" issued to the Sisters telling them not to participate in
the murders seems to have been "quite unnecessary," although he admits
to being aware of one such case in the city of Trier. But since the "file deal-
ing with the Hutthurm branch of the Sisters of Mercy . . . shows no entries
in this regard," he concludes that the "abortions seem all the more
unlikely." And after the parish files labeled "HUTTHURM II, 4A: CULTURAL
AND PASTORAL ISSUES" brought no results, he interpreted this as a confir-
mation of the "defectiveness" of my information. Moreover, he stressed:
"I cannot imagine women of the cloth having participated in abortions."
But even "if one were to assume that the Sisters did participate in abortions, one would have to further assume . . . that the diocesan authorities
would not have brought this kind of situation to the attention of the public—this is, however, exactly what they did." It has become quite easy at
times to neatly do away with one's own history. Dr. Wurster concluded his
four-page letter to me, dated 5 June 1992, with an admonishing remark,
saying that, "an applicant must respect certain . . . reasonable limitations
when accessing the archive . . . in deference to helping the archive maintain its functionality."

I set out to find witnesses. A simple glance into the phone book was all
it took to find the name of Luise Clarenz. Now deceased, she was Dr.
Clarenz's widow and still lived in Hutthurm. However, she did not want
to comment on any of the cases. Her three children declined as well, saying they did not want to "stir up the whole mess once more." For once the
PNP gave me access to their archives, and there I found five articles deal-
ing with the murders of children in Hutthurm. The most rewarding
avenue of all, though, turned out to be my research in the Bavarian state
archive in Landshut, where I came across a complete file on the Hutthurm
hospital, including detailed materials about the abortions. Dr. Sendlinger,

the archivist in charge, knew immediately what I was referring to, and within minutes the expert personnel presented me with the materials that have so summarily been forgotten in the Passau region. In addition, the National Archives in Washington, D.C., hold the investigation reports conducted by the CIC; these files are freely accessible to anyone who requests them.

Sallach, Gangkofener Strasse, Number 7: Strangers Not Wanted

I was first made aware of the former "baby farm" in Sallach in February 1992, by an anonymous caller. It was "a disgrace," he said, that to this day "not a single cross or memorial" marked the site. He suggested that I do some research and "write something about it, preferably an article for the newspaper, so that finally people will know about what happened there."

About fifty kilometers south of Passau lies the city of Eggenfelden. Continuing another twelve kilometers in the direction of Taufkirchen past the village of Rimbach, one reaches Sallach. Sallach is a tiny village of just a few farms and some single-family homes. On the right side of the street an inn belonging to the Rothenaicher family still stands, and diagonally across is the large house of Ernst Denk: "Gangkofener Street, number 7." Most of the villagers are aware of what once happened here. I am not allowed to take photographs, as the owner, Ernst Denk, is yelling at me from afar, beside himself with rage. I ask myself, "What is this man afraid of?" Curious strangers are apparently not wanted here at Gangkofener Street, number 7. I am not even allowed to take a look at the courtyard, despite my very polite request.

If one asks questions here about Sallach or about the baby farm, strange expressions come over people's faces: irritation, distrust, dismay. They offer no explanations for their expressions. When I ask for directions, however, everyone seems to know the way to the baby farm and are even willing to point it out for me. It is only then that they begin to ask questions: Am I going to write an article about the baby farm? Am I looking for someone specific? After all, they say, this happened a long time ago, the story with the baby farm. As I am making inquiries about the history of this institution, I come across bits and pieces of information that fit together surprisingly well. Only twice are my questions met by the door being slammed in my face, accompanied by the comment: "We want nothing to do with that!"

19

Decades ago, the property at Gangkofener Street, number 7, belonged to Xaver Rothenaicher, a farmer in Sallach, who had been one of the few residents who had stood up to the National Socialists and who wanted nothing to do with them or the SA. His actions did not remain without consequence. In 1933, he and his friend Josef Gruber were abducted by SA henchmen. They tied them to a tree and proceeded to beat them with a sort of crude leather cat-o'-nine-tails, with lead weights attached to the ends of the tassels. Xaver Rothenaicher collapsed, his body covered with blood. Shortly afterwards he was deported to Dachau, where he was held for eight weeks. As soon as the war broke out he was drafted into the armed services. His brother Leonhard continued to work on his farm inasmuch as he was able, but soon he too was ordered to the front and the place stood deserted.

Kazimiera Wronska recalls how she, together with her husband, Kazimier, her brother Waclaw Balckyga, and her neighbor Eugeniusz Gronczewski were captured "during a man-hunt" in the vicinity of Warsaw and deported to Germany.

When our train arrived in Eggenfelden, the local farmers were already there waiting to pick up the new forced laborers. My husband and I were assigned to a man named Xaver Rothlehner. Others were already working at the farm; Ms. Palaska, an old Ukrainian woman, and Michal Gudzan, who was also from the Ukraine. And there were two Germans as well, but they did not live with us. My husband and I were forced to work very hard in the fields and at the house, as Xaver Rothlehner had returned from the war seriously wounded in 1918 and could not do any more work himself. He kept telling us that after the German victory all foreigners would be killed. It was not until he finally died that we fared better; his wife was kinder.

Murder Ward: Baby Farm

Karl Steiger from the hamlet of Staudach, near the hamlet of Massing and only a stone's throw from Sallach, was a well-known and fairly influential member of the SA. The abandoned farmhouse that had belonged to the Rothenaicher family was confiscated under his supervision. He had it refurnished with a few beds and other basic necessities. In November 1943, the former agricultural farm became the Sallach "baby farm."

At least 120 women from Poland, the Ukraine, and White Russia were forced to give birth there. They were told that this was a home for newborns with foreign mothers and that their babies would be sheltered and well cared for there so that the women could go back to work "without distraction." I made my first inquiries about surviving children and parents at the Rimbach Inn, located just a few houses down the street from the infamous baby farm. There I was referred to the former assistant mayor, Herr Lautenbacher. He, in turn, sent me to see Elsa Kerscher. When I met her, she invited me in. She opened up an old photo album and found a picture showing the figures of three POWs. She pointed at one of them: "This one, the Pole Stanislaw Kokoszenko, he visited us many times." Frau Kerscher's mother was Swiss and had offered to let Kokoszenko and others listen to forbidden foreign radio broadcasts at her house. For years, the Kerscher home had been *the* meeting place for such activities.

At the end of November 1943, Stanislaw Kokoszenko visited the Kerschers with his girlfriend and their four-month-old baby boy. Elsa remembers: "He was a beautiful baby, strong and healthy. He was sucking on a pacifier, and in his carriage he had a hot-water bottle to keep him warm." She recalls the couple's desperation as they told her about the order they had received to bring their son to the baby farm. The farmer for whom Kokoszenko's girlfriend was working had offered to have the child cared for at the house, but the request was denied. A few days later, on 22 November 1943, the little boy was dead. During that time, a child was dying at the baby farm about every three days. After the war, Stanislaw Kokoszenko immigrated to Toronto; Elsa never heard from him again. But she still was in contact with another former forced laborer, Janina Bury. The two women regularly exchanged letters, and Janina Bury had even visited Elsa in Sallach.

"They knew that they would never see their children again," says Xaver Rothenaicher. "When the women were brought here in the horse-drawn carriages by the farmers they were all crying. They were asking, begging, to be allowed to give birth at the farms where they worked. But this kind of permission was never given." In most cases when the women went into labor, the midwife Kathi Schandl was ordered to come from Gangkofen, a village about eight kilometers away, to assist with the births. She could not bear witness about that time, as she died a few years earlier. Her sister Anna Maria, however, seems to remember that the children did not die from either the heat or the cold: "They were systematically neglected up there."

Joseph Röhrnböck and the SA member Karl Steiger were employed at the baby farm as wardens; among other things they were responsible for the food supply. Several eyewitnesses have testified that many of the women begged desperately for permission to take their babies home with them. Some farmers were prepared to have "their" worker's child grow up in their own families to avoid this separation of mother and child. However, the party never allowed it. On the contrary: the women were forced to hand over to the baby farm all of their other children as well.

None of Them Were There for Very Long

Theoretically it was possible for the mothers to visit their children on some weekends. The reality, however, was different. Those witnesses who are still alive today claim that newborns were fed spoiled milk, resulting in severe diarrhea, and in most cases the babies died after a few days. Older children of three or four experienced more prolonged suffering, often over the course of weeks, before finally dying as well. "There were some beautiful children among them, such beautiful children. But whenever we would return there would be new children, new faces, different children. None of them were there for very long," recalls Xaver Rothlehner Jr., son of Xaver Rothlehner Sr. and a farmer from the neighboring hamlet of Brandstetten, in an interview from 2 May 1992.

He also remembered a woman named Vera, from White Russia, who was there to care for the children. But it was said she was not "quick" enough. She was thus transferred and assigned to work on his father's farm instead; "his" Polish worker, Kazimiera Wronska, was "reassigned" to help at the baby farm. Kazimiera Wronska recalls:

My daughter Maria was born at the hospital. When she was six weeks old, she, too, was to be transferred to the baby farm in Sallach. I knew that all the children there died and so I asked for permission to work there, to be with my daughter. I was allowed to go, and I nursed my daughter there for four months. There were two other women who worked with me: a Russian woman with her two children, Michal and Kati; her husband was missing and she was very despondent. Then there was Vera, from the Ukraine; she was quite a bit older and was the most influential among us with the authorities. For instance, she was authorized to grant permission to parents to take their children home for a day or so. There was also a German cook who lived there. After a provisional delivery room was set up, a midwife came by every once in a

22

while. All the children died from diarrhea. Each child received its food from a special bottle. The only children who survived were the ones that were given food their parents had brought in.

When asked whether the food provided by the baby farm was in fact spoiled, Herr Wronski nodded his head: "Yes, yes," he said, "that's very possible!"

After four weeks, Kazimiera Wronska was replaced by Palaska, the woman from the Ukraine who was old and sick and not able to do heavy farm work any longer.

> The storekeeper and his wife, who had their business across the street from the baby farm, "assisted" with some of the tasks, for instance, by taking the dead children to the cemetery. The graves were nothing more than large holes in the ground that remained loosely covered with wooden planks. Only when the grave was filled with bodies was it covered with earth and closed up.

Women in slave labor from three different districts were brought together as a group in Sallach. This is how the communities Griesbach, Pfarrkirchen, and Eggenfelden disposed of their "children of foreign descent." Dr. Oswald from Gangkofen issued the death certificates. Otto Haas, from Sallach, recalls how as a child he followed behind the sexton on numerous occasions and then watched the funerals. "Of course" people had their suspicions, he said, but nobody "really knew for sure." To this day, they wonder whether everything was indeed pure coincidence or, in fact, intentional.

While home from the front on leave, Xaver Rothenaicher, who had been stationed in Russia during the war years, asked the doctor some questions about what was happening in Sallach. According to Rothenaicher, Dr. Oswald

> did not know how to respond. He told me that he had tried to intervene on a number of occasions. But the party had not allowed it. He was given strict orders not to interfere. The party simply wouldn't let him. The only person they trusted was the midwife, Kathi Schandl. She had access to the home, whereas Dr. Oswald didn't. All they wanted from him was to sign the death certificates. Those in the party wanted all the children dead, they knew what was happening and didn't do anything about it.

Karl Steiger, member of the SA, warned the neighbors not to have any kind of contact with the employees at the baby farm. After all, they, too, were forced laborers, as were the mothers of the children—furthermore, they were all "enemies" of the German people. Leonhard Rothenaicher, however, continued to go there to "check out" what was going on at the baby farm. When he asked how "all this" was possible, neither Vera nor Kazimiera Wronska volunteered any answers. "They were very evasive," he said. "They didn't say anything. They were too frightened. They just ignored me. The only way I can explain it is that they were forced to do so, and they were just very afraid." Anna Haas, also from Sallach, remembered how "none of us were able to have any direct contact with the women; they barely spoke German, anyway. And, regardless, they always left after a few days."

Where to Dispose of the Bodies?

Herr Beslmeisl, the priest from the neighboring community of Reicheneibach, refused to bury "alien offspring" in his small parish graveyard. And there was no graveyard in Sallach. As soon as the first child had died, Beslmeisl wrote a letter to the district administrator of Eggenfelden, who immediately directed a request to the local Staatliches Gesundheitsamt (state health offices) asking them to find an appropriate piece of land in Sallach in which to bury the dead children.

On 8 January 1944, the church administrations of Reicheneibach and Sallach issued a unanimous declaration, according to which the Reicheneibach cemetery "was in no way to be used for the extraordinary and irregular accommodation of corpses originating from the baby farm." Extending the cemetery to accommodate the bodies was "in this time of war, out of the question . . . especially to accommodate foreigners. Within just a few weeks as many as four corpses from the Sallach baby farm . . . have been registered. Due to limited space, the coffins had to be buried one atop the other."

A request was then submitted for the establishment of a "provisional" graveyard directly adjacent to the baby farm. The request read as follows:

> All that is needed is a piece of unused land, surrounded by a fence and marked with a simple cross. At a later date, this graveyard can be made available for commercial use. . . . The site is to be maintained . . . by those who founded the baby farm. Thus, it is the responsibility of the local farmers' association to ensure burial of their dead. In order for this to go forward, steps must be taken before the coming spring.

Three days later, Frau Haas requested that this plan be abandoned; after all, she argued, three major water pipes were located directly under the site of the proposed graveyard. The pipes led directly to her home, and people were concerned about potential poisoning resulting from the decomposing corpses. Moreover, the location of the graveyard at the entrance to the village might scare away potential visitors. Nevertheless, the church administrators informed the ecclesiastic chapter presided over by the bishop in Regensburg, and it was determined that a graveyard would be established in Sallach. On 7 February 1944, local representatives challenged this decision and repeated their request "anew and in the most urgent terms," since "it was to be expected" that there would be at least one death each week. "Once the facility is fully occupied," they continued, "the number may well be higher. In addition, the population is upset about the fact that the bodies of these Polish and Russian children . . . are to be buried in our graveyard, and the citizens demand that this impossible situation be resolved."

After an on-site inspection on 25 February, it was concluded that a piece of land sixty square meters in size located directly next to the baby farm was to be utilized. Father Beslmeisl "requested a quick resolution of the matter . . . due to the many instances of death at the facility," where, "in the month of February alone . . . eleven children and one young mother have died, a situation which necessitates more funerals than we have had in our village throughout the entire year."

By 12 April, the situation had, according to reports, become "even more unbearable and impossible. . . . During the month of March alone," the report continued, "seventeen children have died. In spite of the mass graves it has become impossible to accommodate any more corpses. . . . As the snows have since melted, additional steps are now urgently requested." Otherwise, "the graveyard administration would have to refuse to accept any more bodies." In April, an additional ten children died; on 4 May, Beslmeisl again wrote to the district administration. On 9 June 1944, after another five weeks had passed, the district building authority chose an additional piece of land at a more remote location. According to information found in Report 164, register 4, fascicle 213, number 2164, StAL, on 14 July 1944, the mayor of Sallach informed the district administration that "an emergency cemetery has at this point been established."

The New Graveyard Was Soon Filled Up

Rudolf Salzer, the current parish priest of Reicheneibach, looked up the birth and death registries of his community: sixty-six children from the baby farm have been entered into the baptismal registry, 114 children have been documented in the death records; according to estimates from some eyewitnesses, the number is closer to two hundred. Their parents have been entered as well: women in forced labor and prisoners of war. These children were all they had; they represented their future.

Their pain must have been unimaginable when they were forced to attend their children's funerals so shortly after their birth, knowing that they had been murdered. A woodworker from Reicheneibach named Vilsmeier made the coffins. A sexton named Sedlmeier picked up the tiny corpses. Xaver Rothlehner still recalls how Herr Sedlmeier loaded the tiny coffins onto the rack of his old bicycle to pedal them to the graveyard at Reicheneibach. POWs were then forced to carry the coffins to the grave site, where the coffins were buried in a hasty ceremony by either the priest or the sexton. In the beginning, each child received its own grave, but after seventy or eighty deaths, the "children's graveyard" was already filled to capacity, and after that the corpses had to be buried in Sallach. "[There were] about thirty children and two women," said current owner of the property, Otto Haas, in an interview from 2 May 1992 in Sallach. He still remembers how the two women were buried: "On top of their coffins they placed some money, a piece of sausage, and some bread. A kind of funeral gift, to accompany them on their way." Nobody was familiar with this ritual, but apparently it was tolerated by the locals: "Different people, different customs," the locals were heard to remark. "That's probably the way they do it in Poland and Russia." If one considers the severe food shortages during the final months of the war and the high mortality rate due to malnutrition—especially among the forced labor workers—it is quite surprising that people were not more resentful of this custom, especially since everyone later witnessed how the dogs and cats came to the graves and dug up the food.

On 27 April 1945, the last child died in Sallach. Crib fever was rampant at the baby farm. After several women had succumbed to the disease within a very short period of time, the NSDAP finally reacted, as the deaths had begun to represent a significant loss of cheap labor. The remaining women were transported to the hospital in Eggenfelden, where they gave birth. It is said that no children ever died there. On 3 May 1945, the Americans arrived; on 4 May Kazimiera Wronska got her daughter back. Only about twenty children were still alive.

At that time, Frau Wronska was pregnant with her second child. She and her family took the train home; the journey through Czechoslovakia lasted an entire week. Vera, who was engaged to a man from Poland, accompanied them until they reached the border. In Dziedzice the Wronskis received their papers as well as two hundred zlotys of "start-up capital" —just enough for them to buy something to eat. In 1992, the Wronskis had five children, thirteen grandchildren, and six great-grandchildren. Kazimiera had serious heart disease, and her husband was suffering from stomach cancer. Both joined an association founded four years earlier that soon thereafter counted 40,000 members, called The Association of Polish Victims of the Third German Reich. Dr. Karlo Heßdörfer, who previously served as president of the Bavarian office of restitution, wrote in June 1992:

> At the time of my departure [from my position as office president], the issue of "restitution for the forced labor workers" had yet to be satisfactorily resolved. The forced laborers were not included in the restitution agreement because they had not been persecuted for either of the three reasons specified in paragraph 1 (race, religion, ideology). The perspective here had been that forced labor was a condition "inherent to the state of war" and thus belonged to the category of "reparation" instead of "restitution"; countries, alone, can have a claim to "reparations"; individual persons are excluded. . . . Industry, as well as the German Federal Government, have proven themselves to be anything but generous in the question of the forced laborers. This is sad, but true.

Gemütlichkeit Graveyard

Erika Haas remembers well how, in her childhood, she spent quite a lot of time with her peers at the "Polish graveyard." This is what the locals in Sallach call the place where children and women from the baby farm were buried. In earlier days, village kids planted flowers on the graves. And for a long time, a cast iron cross marked the site. Nobody remembers who put it there. Each grave used to have its own simple wooden cross. "There were about thirty of them," recalls Erika Haas. "Originally, the graveyard was fenced in by a simple wire fence, but that eventually fell apart. And the wooden crosses have rotted away; nobody bothered to try and save them. The people buried there didn't have any relatives to care for the graves." "In the '50s," says Otto Haas, "the community sold the property to my father." He removed the rotten fence and planted saplings all over the small area. "It was not farmable land, with all the bodies in the ground. And besides, it's built on a downhill slope. You can see that for yourself: it's not easy to access." Today, a birch tree grows out of the women's mass grave, another one stands right next to it. A cast iron cross had stood directly atop the graves. Haas Sr. had it removed. According to Erika Hass, in an interview conducted on 2 May 1992 in Sallach, he did so because "It was all rusty, it looked shabby; people could have hurt themselves on it."

In 1972, Otto Haas built a small weekend vacation cottage next to the graves. A wooden plaque with the words *Zur Gemütlichkeit* (cozy cottage) written in red paint hangs directly above the entrance. Right next to it are some benches made from tree trunks. When asked if the history of the place did not make them feel odd, Frau Haas shrugs her shoulders, slightly uncomfortably: "Of course, at first. When we would go down to sit there in the evenings with a bottle of wine it did feel a little creepy. But not any more. We go there to have a drink every now and then. Sometimes we even raise a toast [to those buried there]: 'Cheers, ladies! Cheers!'"

The Children of Barhof, Number 3

Traveling south from Passau on the B 12 federal highway in the direction of Pocking, one comes across the exit to Ruhstorf, after about twenty kilometers. From there a lightly traveled country road leads through the villages of Trostling and Kleeberg to Hader, a small community consisting of farmhouses, a single local inn, a church, and the church cemetery. There, I was told, was where I should begin my search for the gravestone of Max Simonovic, a Polish child. The first thing I noticed when I got to the Hader cemetery was a freshly renovated crypt. Rudolf von Moreau, a fighter pilot who was highly decorated by the Nazis, is buried there. After his death he was honored with a stately funeral; a street close to the cemetery was even renamed after him. The headstone of his grave is marked by five swastikas located just underneath his name, and I noticed that they obviously had been polished quite recently. In 1989, on the occasion of the fiftieth anniversary of his death, the *PNP* published a long panegyric about his career as a pilot. His popularity seems to have remained to this day. Directly opposite of Rudolf von Moreau's crypt I found a small, overturned gravestone. The name engraved on it was barely legible: Max Simonovic, died 19 March 1944. He lived less than three years.

A forgotten grave, and, as I was to find out later, not the only one of its kind in this cemetery.

Following the traces of the Simonovic boy lead me to the tiny hamlet of Barhof, a few kilometers north of Hader. Barhof consists of no more than three houses; visitors hardly ever come here. The people who live here told me that about fifty years ago, "murders were taking place non-stop." The victims were infants and children. Nobody ever inquired about the perpetrators, nor have they to this day. The NSDAP local group leader, Probsteder, was owner of Barhof, number 3. At the end of 1943, the property was "transformed" into a "children's home," an institution parallel to the Sallach baby farm.

Theresia Rell lived for a number of years only a hundred meters outside of Barhof, number 3. Today she still remembers the women who came to her house, most in the late stages of pregnancy, asking for directions to Barhof, number 3. And she still recalls the desperation in their faces.

According to official entries in the registry office, the mayor of Ruhstorf, Herr Hallhuber, states that forty-three children of Polish and Russian women in forced labor were born at Barhof, number 3. Thirty-two of them were reported to have died either within a few days, or at the latest after four weeks, following birth. In addition, another fifty-seven dead children who had been born outside the children's home, but who were transferred there afterwards, were registered.

Eyewitnesses are certain that in reality about three hundred children had lost their lives at Barhof, number 3, and that Probsteder had reported only a fraction of that number. This is entirely possible. In the book titled *Schreiberinnen des Todes* (Female writers of death), it is claimed, for instance, that several Polish women who were employed at the registry in Auschwitz reported that only one name would be entered in the registries when in fact numerous women had arrived. The official causes of death usually ranged from diarrhea, to severe vomiting, to liver failure. In *Schreiberinnen des Todes* it is stated that those responsible for providing this information had to choose from a list of ten to fifteen official causes, which in many cases in no way reflected the real cause of death. Alois Stöckl tells me that his father used to deliver milk next door at Barhof, number 3. The milk was subjected to strict controls, so it could not have been because of the quality of the milk that so many children died there so quickly. Katharina Huber, the neighbor on the other side of the property, is not prepared to talk about Barhof, number 3. In a 11 July 1992 interview with other neighbors, however, I was told somewhat cryptically that her mother frequently went there to "deliver" things. According to eyewitness reports, approximately thirty to forty foreign female forced laborers were employed at the Kleeberg estate, situated just a few kilometers from Barhof. When the Polish couple Maria and Stefan were expecting their child, the young mother, witnesses say, fought "tooth and nail" to avoid being committed to Barhof, number 3. Finally, Baroness von Moreau asked her employee Maria Kurz if she might be able to take care of the baby during the day; the helpful young woman immediately responded that she would. This way the forced laborer Maria was able to deliver her baby at the estate, then give her child, Kazimierz Aleksander, to his foster mother. Maria was back performing hard labor harvesting the fields just one day after having given birth. That this was expected seemed to have upset many of the women. They were afraid this beautiful woman might hemorrhage and die; but she was not allowed to rest. The property manager at Kleeberg was known for his cruelty, and he made sure that his foreigners worked as hard as possible. Abuse and beatings were a daily occurrence. When the Americans marched in, he hid from them behind the altar of the church, a fact the town elders still recall with a smirk.

In May 1945, Maria and Stefan returned to Poland with their son Kazimierz Aleksander. Shortly after the end of the war she sent a letter to the people at the Kleeberg estate. Nobody could read it, however, as it was written in Polish. A few decades later, in 1991, two Polish men arrived at the castle of Kleeberg, asking for the family who had brought up little Kazimierz Aleksander. But the current owners of the castle claimed to know nothing about the child and sent the men away. Marianne Bicsancyk, the daughter of Maria Kurz, was extremely distraught by this. As a young girl she had changed the little boy's diapers many times and she is certain that he was one of the men. She would have loved to find out what had become of him and his family.

Access to Files Denied

Reinhard Hofer lives in Hütting, barely a kilometer from Barhof. He works for the International Tracing Service of the Red Cross in Munich and has long been interested in the events that took place at Barhof, number 3. "There's simply not much to be found out," he says, "nobody really tried to prevent these things from happening back then; they just watched them happen. And the local administrator, Probsteder, committed suicide a few weeks after the war was over." No de-Nazification of those respon-sible had ever taken place. All the victims were dead, and their parents had since fled and resettled in various places across the globe. Apparently nobody was interested in solving this particular case. In any event, no one among the local population has ever come forward and reported it. And without a rightful plaintiff, the district attorney would not prosecute.

A senior government official of the district of Griesbach, Andreas Mangold, was head of the police division for foreigners from 1941 to 1945. He was a member of the Nazi Party and belonged to the SA as well as eight other organizations. According to a report published on page six of the 18 December 1948 issue of the *PNP*, the chief incriminating evi-dence against him before the courts was his treatment of foreign workers in forced labor, "whom he had, in many cases . . . abused, denounced to the Gestapo, or ensured the deportation of to concentration camps, which occasionally resulted in their death." In 1946 he was indicted as an "insti-gator" and sentenced to three years in a labor camp; he lost his fortune as a result. According to a report in the *PNP* from 9 February 1949, a retrial had taken place in 1948. It was not possible to determine the result of this trial. The *PNP* announced in large type: "MANGOLD CLAIMS TO ONLY HAVE SLAPPED WORKERS."

In the case of Albert Steger, the retired district administrator and Man-gold's former superior, it was concluded that he had not been instrumen-tal in the death of workers, but that he had simply occasionally slapped Polish laborers and "locked them up for one to two days, giving them only water and bread." Furthermore, he had protected three French prisoners of war "from punishment" and allowed them to listen to foreign broad-casts. However, he was categorized as an activist and was sentenced to two years in a labor camp, due to the fact, that, according to a report in the 18 December 1948 issue of the *PNP*, "he misused his position as senior Nazi to allow transgressions."

According to an article published on page three of the 4 May 1948 "Rottal Rundschau" regional edition of the *PNP*, Johannes Andreas Ram-mensee, the former NSDAP district administrator of Griesbach, Pfar-rkirchen, and Eggenfelden, was deemed an accomplice and tried in 1948, whereby he was sentenced to four years in labor camp. Fifty percent of his property was to be confiscated. Andreas Rammensee had been an SA stan-dard bearer, as well as a member of the NSDAP and other organizations. He was instrumental in "the arrest of 150 people," and was characterized

as a fanatic Nazi by an eyewitness. Owing to his age, however—Rammensee
was sixty-seven years old—the court recommended a plea for mercy and
assured him of its support.

Evidence indicates that all of these people were involved in the events
that took place at Barhof, number 3. The district court of Passau, however, prevented any attempts to determine this for certain. For a long time
I was denied access to these court files, and eventually it was claimed that
the files "no longer exist."

One Gravestone for Ninety Children

For decades any search for a grave site at the Hader cemetery to com-
memorate the children murdered at Barhof, number 3, would have been
in vain. The priest Anton Huber, who has now been head of the parsonage for several years, changed this. "There is so much to do, I don't know
where to begin," he said apologetically. "But the gravestone for the Polish
child should be finished by the end of this year." That was over a decade
ago now. In the mean time the engraving is again barely legible.

When Anton Huber arrived in Hader, Theresia Rell told him about the
people who were constantly inquiring about the children's home. He
searched the cemetery and finally found the headstone to the grave of
three-year-old Max Simonovic. He was the only one to survive infancy
at Barhof, number 3, probably because his father had been involved in
the administration of the home. Twice within the last two decades the
headstone had been moved because they were running out of space for
new graves. Huber found out where the original grave had been located.
He planned to have the engravings on the stone renewed and to add an
inscription stating that here, at the Hader cemetery, ninety more victims
of the mass murder committed against "offspring of alien descent" lay
buried. When I talked with him in the summer of 1992, he was still
not exactly certain about the precise wording and design, but he had discussed the plan with the church administration and they had agreed to
it "without reservation." Needless to say, perhaps, this plan never fully
materialized.

When I asked Anton Huber why he had initially become so involved in
the matter, he answered without hesitation: "This must not be forgotten.
Even today, many people don't know about these events any more. They
have almost vanished from memory. Perhaps the home was never much
talked about from the very beginning. But these were human beings like

you and me, even if they weren't locals. The victims, these children, must never be forgotten. And ultimately it must be said that the people who lived here took part in what was happening." On the German National Day of Mourning in 1992, the town of Hader finally received its memorial. The old stone was polished, given a fresh inscription, and placed at the entrance to the cemetery.

Barhof, Number 3, Today: Red Roses in Gelatin

In the 1970s, a commune acquired the property at Barhof, number 3, for 40,000 deutschmarks. It was partially renovated and changed owners soon after that. It was then bought by Sophie von Behr, a former journalist, together with another woman; they planned to spend "the twilight of their lives" there. Neither of them claimed to have been aware of the history of the place and proceeded to renovate it further, bit by bit. On the occasion of a village celebration in 1988 they happened to overhear some of the locals talking about the murders of the children. "If you ask me, there is something like a curse on a house where such things happened. There have always been problems there, even with the former owners."

All total, eighty-nine children had been murdered at the site where the women live today. Sophie von Behr says that she "often has nightmares" about the events. In her diary, she made an entry in black ink saying that she had just visited the Hader graveyard, where she had laid twenty-seven roses on the graves. She showed me the basement, where the children's coffins had been piled up, to be used when needed. Pacifiers were allegedly still found there after the war was over. Sophie von Behr enjoys entertaining. On 21 June 1992 she invited twelve women to celebrate summer solstice at Barhof, number 3. She asked all the women to dress in red or violet-colored clothes. She had pronounced the motto for the evening to be "Flesh and Blood." She was hoping her guests would "bring contributions in the spirit of fire, blood, flesh, sun, light, and dance—flesh and blood in the sense of something strong and alive and natural." Thus inspired, one of the women brought an arrangement of "red roses in gelatin"; "wine, blood and earth were mixed together and herbal blood tonics" were prepared. The invitation read: "This year we shall dance and stomp around . . . " Sophie von Behr herself decided to enact the theme of the forced labor women giving birth. She had gotten hold of the death records of the eighty-nine murdered children and suggested that they be read. There were rose stems and piles of red rose petals on the table, illuminated by red light. Before Sophie von Behr was ready to light up a bonfire for the solstice celebration, she encouraged her guests to help her come to terms with the history of the forced labor women and their dead children.

Whether such an esoteric circle can help to accomplish such a task is doubtful. The chances, even for a serious attempt at reconciliation, are generally very bad. The mayor of Ruhstorf, Herr Hallhuber, claims that the documents for the years between 1933 and 1945 have "disappeared." According to him, any evidence that might offer clues to the events that took place in this community and, specifically, to what happened at Barhof, number 3, have been "erased." Further research is not on the agenda, and within a few more years even the last remaining eyewitnesses will have died.

CHAPTER 2

The Plattling Camp

About forty kilometers northwest of Passau, in Lower Bavaria, lies the small town of Plattling. About 12,000 people live there today, most of whom are employed by local industry. According to the 17 October 1946 issue of the Mittelbayerische Zeitung, *during the war Plattling was the site of a work camp operating under supervision of the Todt organization; in 1944 it was converted into a concentration camp. Wilhelm Weber, a local farmer, believes the camp was located at the site that today houses the buildings of the Schreiner wood manufacturing plant.*

According to page fifty-nine of a 1991 bulletin from the Historische Heimatblätter series titled "Die KZ-Aussenkommandos des KZ-Lagers Flössenburg: Ganacker und Plattling" (The Ganacker and Plattling sub-commandos of the Flössenburg concentration camp), edited by Georg Artmeier, in 1944 the concentration camp prisoners were forced to lay the foundation for a large hangar where jet fighter planes were to be constructed. Until then the planes had been housed in the neighboring town of Hettenkofen. The hangar was camouflaged to look like an agricultural building. It was built adjacent to the Weber's farm so that it could survive the war without being targeted by bombs. The airport in Höhenrain, on the outskirts of Plattling, was to be rebuilt to allow for the deployment of a fighter squadron as well as the use of a newly developed turbine fighter jet. In 1940 the area consisted of approximately 270 acres. Farmers who voluntarily offered their fields were promised ten times more land in Poland and the Ukraine once the final victory had been achieved. Farmers who did not cooperate were dispossessed.

As found on page fifty-one of the Artmeier bulletin, the entire airport complex, which covered an area approximately the size of the industrial district between Plattling and Michaelsbuch, two kilometers away, was declared off limits for civilians. It was never completed. The prison camp itself was hermetically sealed off. Anybody who approached the prisoners was severely reprimanded by SS men, and even threatened. Karl Fischer, then a boy of fourteen who is quoted on page fifty-eight of the bulletin, remembers:

> Sometime in the year 1944 I saw some of these prisoners; they had to cart manure at the old Wagner farm right across from the Fürther Keller restaurant. They had a heavy cart with broad, iron wheels. After it had been loaded with the manure, the prisoners harnessed themselves to the wagon and began pulling. But it wasn't working. For one thing, the prisoners were extremely weak. Also, the heavy cart was stuck in a sewage ditch next to the dung heap and it was very difficult to pull it out. The prisoners were chained together but weren't able to move forward. Finally I offered to get a pair of oxen and a harness. But the SS man who was supervising the prisoners pushed me aside and started to yell at me. He said if I wanted to harness anything I could start by harnessing myself to the other prisoners. I'll always remember the sight.

On 20 February 1945 the number of concentration camp prisoners at Plattling saw a dramatic increase. The old schoolhouse behind the parish church St. Magdalena was fenced off with barbed wire. The new arrivals were already familiar with life at a concentration camp. The following report appeared in the 8 October 1946 issue of the *Isarbote* newspaper:

> They came from Flossenbürg, one of the most cruel of concentration camps in which all 30,000 prisoners had to line up naked in the yard on a freezing January morning to endure yet another roll call. Five hundred of the prisoners were pronounced fit for work, loaded on a cattle wagon, and transported to Plattling. There they were to build, under the supervision of forty SS men and four SS officers, the runway for [Hermann] Göring's final airplanes; as the Allies had drawn closer, the remaining planes of the Luftwaffe, of which Göring was commander, had been moved further and further away from the front, and Passau, located as it is at the border with Austria, was literally at the end of the line. For the first days there was nothing to eat at all, because there was still no kitchen at the camp in which to cook anything; later they received a liter of broth after work as a sort of combined lunch and dinner.

On 8 October 1946, under the headline "MEMORIAL FOR THE VICTIMS OF THE PLATTLING CONCENTRATION CAMP," the *Isar Post* newspaper published the following information: "When in February 1945 a convoy of people dressed in black-and-white-striped clothing was chased down from the train station toward the schoolhouse the population did not know from where and why these unfortunates had come to the city."

Prison Life

The Artmeier bulletin describes the conditions of the camp in detail (130). The prisoners were mostly Jews. They came from various countries, mostly from Poland, and were subjected to the most horrible tortures. They had to perform extremely hard labor digging at the airport in Höhenrain and suffered from hunger and illness. Beatings by the SS guards were a daily occurrence. As the concentration camp was located next to the parish church, churchgoers were able to hear routinely the screams of the beaten and abused prisoners. Twice a day the prisoners were escorted through the town of Höhenrain; they worked from sunrise to sunset (121). The prisoners were in such miserable shape that they were barely able to stand up straight, even in the mornings. At four o'clock each morning they had to walk four kilometers to the location where they performed their labor; they wore only very light prison uniforms. The prisoners were forced to repair damage caused by air raids to private homes and on the train station. They also had to work at the post office.

On the way to the airport the prisoners were made to walk in rows of three; the weakest ones were escorted along in the middle of the convoy. Only a few were wearing coats. Sometimes they were also pulling a cart. On their way back the cart was loaded up with the bodies of dead or collapsed prisoners, thrown on top of each other (57). The ones who were no longer able to walk back to the camp were pushed on wheelbarrows by the other prisoners. On those occasions when the prisoners were assigned to perform labor in public, the SS men worked together with the Plattling police force to oversee the operation (54). Adolf Weber, who as a boy worked as a runner for the civilian air defense, had to take the prisoners to their assigned locations, escorted by the SS, because the SS men did not know the way (128). On one occasion he was ordered to take them to a brick factory in the town of Straubing, some fifteen kilometers away, but his grandfather prevented him from doing so because he was outraged at the way the concentration camp inmates were treated. At the beginning of April 1945 the entire Plattling concentration camp, including its kitchen, infirmary, and its staff of guards, was moved to a new site within the drafty halls of the brick factory in Höhenrain, belonging to the farmer Herr Frohnauer.

The brick factory and adjacent buildings that housed the prisoners were surrounded by a three-and-a-half-meter, barbed wire fence. Trained attack dogs patrolled the grounds, making escape impossible. A number of the SS men were quartered at the Waas Inn (52). Frau Frohnauer says that the four or five SS men who were staying in her old potato cellar had been friendly enough. In Höhenrain the prisoners first had to dig a sewage canal, then they had to lay pipes in a gravel pit. Train tracks led from the gravel pit all the way to the airport; the gravel was transported in small wagons along these tracks. Neighbors watched from their houses as prisoners who had been left behind clung to the fence surrounding the camp and wailed with hunger (56).

The prisoners were ordered to transport approximately 10,000 metric tons of cement, which had been brought in in sacks from the train station in Plattling, to Höhenrain and to various local farms. Prisoners who were near total exhaustion were severely beaten or in some cases even killed by the "Kapos"—inmates (usually political prisoners) who were put in charge of the other prisoners. One of the SS men was particularly brutal. He was short and fat and spoke with a Viennese dialect. He used to sic a vicious dog on the weakest prisoners to get them to work. A former inmate testified that either SS men or Kapos were known to slowly beat prisoners to death for the smallest of offenses, and sometimes even killed them by beating them with the legs of chairs or large bones from slaughtered animal carcasses. Frequently several prisoners were simply shot after daily roll call (55). Approximately twenty-five such victims were buried close to the cemetery in Höhenrain. Among them was one who had been shot because he had gotten up one night to relieve himself, another because he had taken too long to do his business. Prisoners who were sick were thrown alive into the latrine. Every escape attempt was punished by death. A man from Czechoslovakia who had taken some leftover meat was killed immediately after being caught. As of 8 April 1945, the 1st SS Train Brigade, also known as the 6th Train Brigade, was also deployed in Plattling (53). The only known fact about this brigade is that as of 13 January 1945 it was under the authority of the Sachsenhausen concentration camp, and that it had been mentioned in an official document.

A list of inmates at the Plattling camp from 13 April 1945 mentions only the names of 449 prisoners. "The prisoners were severely emaciated" (118). The SS finally confiscated a cattle cart from the Schreiner butcher's shop in Plattling to carry away the corpses. In another case the innkeeper

Josef Waas observed how dead bodies were tossed out of a train car and covered with earth in a mass grave opposite the site of today's sugar factory in the northeastern part of Plattling. To this day it has yet to be determined whether or not these were murdered prisoners from the Plattling concentration camp. Yet another mass grave existed next to the gravel pit belonging to the Frohnauer family. Concentration camp victims who had been tortured to death were buried there on a daily basis, the layers of corpses separated by just a thin layer of soil. In other places the dead were simply thrown into a ditch on the side of the road and haphazardly covered with some dirt.

Not Everyone Looked the Other Way

"When the prisoners were marched through the yard," the farmer Wilhelm Weber recalls, "they sometimes bent down to pick up household trash, potato peels and other such things, and ate them up greedily. They had to do this secretly, because if a guard had seen him he would have rammed the butt of his rifle into the nape of their neck." He continued: "Once my father had the opportunity to talk to one of the prisoners. He asked him why he was here. The man replied that he was a doctor and that no one had ever told him the reason for his imprisonment" (133). "Most of them were academics, lawyers, and doctors as well as intellectuals from abroad. Years later one of the prisoners came and visited us" (134).

A few of the residents placed food by the side of the road so that the prisoners could pick it up as they were passing by. One small business in Plattling named Stanglmeier frequently donated broth to the camp. Frau Fanny Schreiner, who has since passed away, remembered:

> Oftentimes we cooked potatoes in the evening, when the prisoners came back. They knew this. We put the potatoes down by the gate so that the prisoners could take them as they were passing. On Sundays we used to ask the supervisors if we could use some of the prisoners to help us chop wood. Of course we did not really need them. . . . Instead we picked up the two or three they let us have and gave them something to eat. That's when we had a chance to talk to them. I remember that one time there was one, a Jew, who was very young. He was only seventeen. (122)

She continued: "My neighbor told me that those prisoners who came down with dysentery were locked away in the attic under the roof and left there to die. Some of them jumped to their death from the window. We talked about this many times" (124).

Frau Frohnauer, who with others witnessed the suffering of the inmates on a daily basis, recalls: "One time, when the prisoners were forced to dig a ditch in front of our house, one of our Polish housekeepers brought them some steamed potatoes she had hidden in her apron. Right away she was scolded by the guards" (117). If the food was discovered, a member of the SS would usually kick it into the dirt or throw it away. Were one of the prisoners to try to go get it, he would be shot immediately. Beatings with rifle butts, oftentimes directly in the face, were a frequent occurrence. Josef Oscar Brauner was one of the perpetrators. Brauner was a member of the Death's Head Regiment of the SS and then a guard at the Dührenfurt work camp, and later in Plattling. He was taken into custody in June 1945. During his questioning by American officials Brauner admitted to having abused inmates of the Plattling concentration camp. A remark in the protocol of the hearing reads: "It is without question that there will be an inquest against the defendant, Herr Brauner, and possibly of other guards of the Flossenbürg concentration camp and its external camps." Whether it ever came to such a proceeding or whether a judgement in this case was ever reached could not be determined.

Anna Stangl from Hettenkofen remembers: "They were transported here in trains, in groups of about fifty to sixty men, with four to six men guarding them. Back then we also had some Russian prisoners here at the farm. . . . The Russians were steaming potatoes in the house. Afterwards, they took loose some of the roof tiles and threw the potatoes to the prisoners, because it was forbidden to hand them anything. It was only the Russians, though, who dared to do such things" (125).

"On our property," says Wilhelm Weber,

> we had Polish and Russian forced laborers. We had a good relationship with them. The prisoners were subjected to the freezing cold being forced to stand outside during lunch. My father tried to convince the major to let the prisoners take shelter in the stables, arguing that it would hardly be helpful to the Wehrmacht if some of the prisoners were to freeze to death. The major warned him to watch what he said, that it could get him in trouble. My father had to be careful because he was generally critical of the party. He was not a member of the NSDAP and did not want to be recruited as a soldier in the Second World War, since he had already served at the front during the First World War. Eventually he prevailed and the prisoners were allowed to spend their lunch time with the cows inside the warm stable. (131)

There they drank cow's milk and ate leftovers that were lying around, such as potatoes and carrots. Because food was rationed and significant amounts of milk had to be delivered to the officials, Weber Sr. informed the prisoners that he could not give them any more milk. Instead he secretly brought them a two-hundred-liter kettle filled with potatoes and a little bit of milk. Wilhelm Weber says: "A Polish woman had to prepare the food. For the prisoners these were the best meals they could have gotten, as the food was high-quality produce." He continued: "It was total chaos when the food was given out for the first time. The prisoners were so hungry that the guards could not restrain them. . . . The guards were beating down the prisoners with their rifle butts, knocking them over as the prisoners ran toward the food. Eventually my father stepped in and pleaded with the guards to stop the beating" (132). Unfortunately their bodies were so unaccustomed to food, having been completely depleted due to malnutrition, that the meals caused severe diarrhea in many of the prisoners. If they needed to relieve themselves they had to go to a gravel pond. Were one of them to go more than once, he would be punished because, in the eyes of the SS, he was simply shirking work. Once, when one of the ponies died and was buried, some of the prisoners attempted to dig up the cadaver in order to eat it. But the SS guards forcefully prevented them from doing so. Polish forced laborers continued to secretly pass out steamed potatoes to the concentration camp prisoners. On one cold day in April, when Weber Jr. drove home a load of beet roots, some of the prisoners jumped up onto his cart and tried to eat the frozen beets.

The Long Death March

On 24 April 1945, the majority of the Plattling camp was evacuated. The SS left as well. Only about twenty to thirty inmates who were unable to walk were left behind. The memorial site of the former Flossenbürg concentration camp displays the route taken from Plattling, through the towns of Aholming, Buchhofen, and Hartkirchen, all the way to Eichendorf. According to the judicial investigation report, however, the convoy marched in a southern direction from Plattling and about thirty kilometers, past Otzing toward Eggenfelden. The first prisoner to collapse was shot and killed just outside of Plattling, in Eschendorf, and then thrown into a ditch by the roadside. The others were driven on; the number of victims increased by the hour. A man from the neighboring village of Kleinweichs was ordered to use his cart to collect the dead. They were simply being thrown into a gravel pit just outside the town. The road from Plattling-Enchendorf to Otzing was literally strewn with corpses. The Americans later made certain that the party members buried them in a mass grave; the grave, however, was abandoned just a few months later.

From Otzing the SS led the prisoners on to Haunerdorf, where they met up with and continued the march together with the survivors of the Ganacker subcamp, located a few kilometers south of Plattling. One broke down and died in Simbach, five in Arnstorf, two in Haunersdorf, and ten more in Schönau. In Eggenfelden yet another one died; five corpses were found in Hirschham, one in Reischach, and another two in Winhöring. Once they arrived in Winhöring they met up with the evacuees marching from the external command of the concentration camp in Regensburg and continued to drag on together. The commander of the Plattling camp deserted the convoy in Mühldorf. In Garching the next corpse was found, followed by one in Tachtering, and another in Trostberg.

It was either on 2 or 3 May—opinions diverge on this point—that American troops liberated a small handful of survivors in Surberg, near Traunstein, approximately one hundred kilometers south of Plattling. Immediately preceding this event, however, two hundred of the prisoners were shot to death by the SS and dumped into a gravel pit just outside Surberg; another sixty-six prisoners were murdered in a forest close to Gleisnetz/Surberg, according to the 9 May 1945 report from the local community administration; on 7 November 1945 the bodies were buried in the local cemetery.

They Were a Horrifying Sight

Some of the people left behind in the Plattling camp were able to escape and to find refuge with farmers in Höhenrain. However, this was extremely risky to everyone involved. If just one of them had been found, potentially all of them would have been shot, prisoners and farmers alike. On page 117 of the Artmeier bulletin, Frau Frohnauer remembers: "Once the Americans had opened the gates to the camp the prisoners just streamed out. They immediately ran toward our wash-house where we were loading up steamed potatoes; they ate them up greedily. I was terribly afraid. They had wounds on their heads and hands; they looked as if they had leprosy. They were a horrifying sight. One of them ended up staying at our farm."

Actually these prisoners were to have been evacuated by the SS as well, but the Americans had been faster. Immediately after the rescue each farmer was assigned a certain number of prisoners and ordered to feed them. Former party members and Nazi functionaries were given more prisoners than others. Occasionally there would be an assault. An eyewitness related the following: "Half a year after the American liberation some of the guards who had been in charge of supervising the camp returned to the Hundsruck Hof inn to meet their girlfriends. There they were surprised by some former concentration camp prisoners. One of the former guards was killed, another one survived by playing dead" (119).

The fence surrounding the camp had to be taken down by the former prisoners (117). According to the October 1946 article in the *Isar Post*, survivors were able to point out locations where corpses had been buried. The eyewitness from the Artmeier bulletin continues: "Some of the prisoners were later treated at one of the hospital barracks. The head nurse contracted typhoid fever and died as a consequence" (121). "A Jew by the name of Rosenzweig was the liaison between the Americans, the Counter Intelligence Corps (CIC) and the former prisoners" (119). According to the 11 January 1946 letter from the mayor to the district administration office in Deggendorf, as early as 1945

> the military government gave orders to establish a separate cemetery for inmates of the concentration camp. The Americans refused to have the concentration camp prisoners buried on the grounds of the existing graveyard, and they also refused to have them honorably buried in a separate section of this graveyard. Instead the occupiers confiscated a piece of property that belonged to Fanny Schreiner and bordered the Straubinger Strasse. All concentration camp inmates who had been unceremoniously covered with earth in the vicinity of Plattling were to be buried in this cemetery.

In December of 1986 the Bavarian Castles, Parks, and Lakes Administration in Plattling informed me that, according to their documents, the dead were exclusively concentration camp prisoners who had died in April 1945 in the area south of Plattling.

The dead of various religions, but predominantly the Jewish dead, were buried there. The few surviving Jews established their own cultural community, which in 1946 still consisted of sixty-six members; at the beginning of the 1950s, however, it disintegrated. In the 29 April 1947 article from the Plattling newspaper, bearing the headline "OBELISK TO COM-MEMORATE OUR JEWISH FELLOW CITIZENS," on 19 January 1947, a presiding committee consisting of five people was elected. All of them had been survivors of the Plattling camp and most of them were in very poor health as a result of their imprisonment.

Only Murders Will Be Prosecuted

German investigators first became interested in the history of the Plattling camp only as late as 1967—for it was then that the remains of one of the victims were found, by accident. An excerpt from the Artmeier bulletin details how in the investigation proceedings for case number 115 Js 4610/76, the courts would rule that "Manslaughter, which includes death by execution, falls under the legal clause of the statute of limitations and, as such, is no longer subject to prosecution. Only murders will be prosecuted if cruel and unusual intention or racial ideology played a prevalent role in the killing. The prosecutor's office limits its work to the task of finding the perpetrator. . . . Since those responsible are no longer to be found alive, the case has been terminated."

The Burden of One's Own History

On 6 March 1946, the Plattling city council decided to erect a memorial at the concentration camp cemetery. Two weeks later a committee was formed for this purpose; it included the cemetery administrator Herr Reichhart, the former concentration camp prisoner Hans Hefele, the Social Democratic Party (SPD) city councilman Lasser, as well as Mayor Weise, who was presiding. In order for the council to be in a position to finance the memorial, Weise, in accordance with the city council members pronounced the following decree:

> In recognition and in honor of the unfortunate human beings who lost their lives as victims of fascism, the city council of Plattling has decided to build a memorial at the site of the local concentration camp cemetery at Straubinger Strasse. This memorial is to be built in a way that honors the victims, with a tasteful setting and the creation of a landscaped garden that will serve as a permanent memorial for generations to come. Naturally funds are needed for the erection and the design of this memorial. The task of raising these funds is not just the responsibility of the city; the entire population and each single individual is called upon to assist in this endeavor. I therefore appeal to the entire population of

the city of Plattling to contribute to this project with individual donations and for each to give as much as he can afford. It is our responsibility and duty to create a place for the victims who lost their lives
because of insane theories and cruelties, and by doing so, to express our
firm and sincere desire to try to make amends, at least symbolically, for
the crimes committed in the name of fascist terror and madness.

Clearly Interested in Making Amends

An article from the 15 October 1946 issue of the *PNP* bearing the headline "187 MARTYRS OF THE BLOODY REGIME" describes the cemetery. It
was located at the northern edge of Plattling, bordering the main road
leading to Straubing. A stone wall with two iron gates separated it from
the street; a hedge was planted forming the borders along the sides and
the back. Several residential buildings were located just a stone's throw
away. According to the mayor's report of 20 July 1948 to the Bavarian
Ministry of the Interior, the graveyard was divided into four approximately equal parts, and each part had its own sarcophagus-like burial
mound decorated with an arrangement of flowers. In the middle stood a
granite obelisk with an engraved inscription in German, Hebrew, English,
and Polish that read, "THIS IS THE RESTING PLACE OF 185 VICTIMS OF FAS-
CISM." It was built upon "a firm foundation of granite" and "inclement
weather conditions would not be able to damage or otherwise topple" the
structure. It was created by the Josef Hingsamer stonemasonry of Plattling.

On 8 October 1946, the *Isar Post* newspaper announced the imminent
unveiling of the memorial "to honor the victims." The headline, in bold
letters, proclaimed that Plattling had "taken an active part through donations of money and time" in its creation and thus proven that they were
clearly interested in making amends. A two-column article followed,
reminding the reader in no uncertain terms of the history of the Plattling
concentration subcamp, which had claimed 185 human lives. The memorial, the *Isar Post* continued, "serves as a constant reminder of the acts of
terror committed under Hitler's bloody regime," and "shall forever remain
a decent memorial."

Obviously the population of Plattling and its vicinity came out in large
numbers for this commemoration, which took place on 13 October 1946.
Among the guests were the American military governor of the neighboring town of Deggendorf, Major W. Hart, as well as officers of the American army, several representatives of the Jewish communities of Bavaria, and

a group of Polish, former concentration camp prisoners. The Ingolstadt newspaper *Donau Kurier* published a slightly clumsy report on the events; the 15 October 1946 issue of the *Isar Post*, bearing the headline "CONCEN- TRATION CAMP MEMORIAL DEDICATED," provided the following, very detailed account:

> After the numerous representatives of the Jewish communities and sev- eral groups of former concentration camp prisoners had taken position with their flags, the mayor of Plattling officially opened the ceremony. In his opening speech Mayor Weise stressed that a large part of the German people had to be considered innocent of the unspeakable acts of cruelty committed by the Nazis, because for a long time the horrible events that took place in Hitler's murder chambers had not been public knowledge. This included the people of Plattling, who were not aware, in the beginning, of the cruelties and the suffering to which the prison- ers were subjected when, in the fall of 1944, they were being marched through the city in their striped prison clothes. When, however, the truth later became known, the majority of the citizens of Plattling were outraged at the inhuman treatment and, in spite of the dangers and strict orders not to do so, gave food to the prisoners.

On that day, the mayor continued, there was little else the people of Plat- tling could do but to create an honorable memorial; the Plattling city council had decided in favor of such a plan in March of that year. The entire population of Plattling and its surroundings had contributed to this project of atonement, through donations and by offering their help. This memorial was to serve as a symbol and a reminder to all generations that such an injustice can never be committed again. Thereupon the mayor unveiled the memorial in the shape of an obelisk, built from local granite, inscribed with the words: "THIS IS THE RESTING PLACE OF 185 VICTIMS OF FASCISM." Mayor Weise and the governor of Deggendorf then proceeded to place wreaths at the base of the monument. Thereafter the memorial was decorated with a large number of additional wreaths. What followed was an address by the representative of the regional committee of Regens- burg, in which the speaker recounted the sufferings and cruelties to which the Jewish people had been exposed during the last twelve years. The gal- lows of Nuremberg, he emphasized in a reference to the Americans' sen- tencing of Nazis to death by hanging at the Nuremberg Trials, could not bring back the dead. However, the German people could seek atonement for the crimes committed against a large part of the Jewish people.

It was therefore necessary to point out to the German administrative authorities not to view those Jews who survived as an onerous remnant, but to instead recognize that we, the Germans, were being presented with a duty and an opportunity to provide restitution to a few for what had cost so many their lives. The Jews, so the speaker said, were without any form of sustenance. In order to overcome their current troubles, they needed help; help they should not have to ask for, but instead, was their full right to demand. In the presence of this memorial, he continued, it was necessary for each single individual to ask himself the question, to what extent he himself bore responsibility for the victims.

The Wheels of Bureaucracy Turn Slowly

As documented in the 20 July 1948 mayoral report to the Bavarian Ministry of the Interior, on 31 October 1946, the mayor of Plattling, Herr Weise, applied to the Bavarian federal ministry for a yearly contribution of 650 reichsmarks to help with the upkeep of the graves. Josef Reichhart, the honorary cemetery administrator, was given responsibility for the care. On 21 September 1947, almost a year later, the federal commissioner Philipp Auerbach informed the mayor that he was prepared "to take over expenses for the graves from members of the United Nations." However, he was not going to pay a flat fee, but instead planned to reimburse them for the money actually spent. Just one month earlier, the district administration had been asked to finally resolve the matter of the property. According to a decree issued by the Bavarian ministry of the interior on 25 May 1948—after another eight months had passed—an inspection of the cemetery was finally scheduled. The participants included, among others, the deputy district administrator, the district building inspector, as well as Herr Levkowiecz, Herr Augenbraun, Herr Smulowiec, and Herr Heuberger from the Plattling Jewish community.

The cemetery was found to be "well cared for." There were no signs of desecration or other damage to the grounds. At worst a few of the inscriptions were found to be slightly faded. The delegation agreed that improvements could be made by planting a few trees such as red beeches, the kind that had been planted next to the memorial itself, directly behind the stone outer wall. In order to ensure proper watering of the plants atop the grave sites it would also be necessary to lay approximately 150 meters of new pipes. First they would have to call for some estimates, and then the costs had to be approved. In the midst of all this activity someone suddenly realized that the land on which the cemetery had been built belonged to Fanny Schreiner. This realization made for more confusion, this time of a financial nature.

However, in order to move ahead a committee was formed, which included Joseph Reichhart, Salomon Augenbraun as well as the mayor, Josef Niebauer. On 11 January 1949, Niebauer again admonished the district administration to resolve the matter of who was the rightful owner of the property. His initial request, which he had submitted approximately a year and a half earlier, had remained unanswered.

Slowly the wheels began to turn. At the end of January the district administrator made an official inquiry to determine the value and size of the property. By the middle of February 1949, Fanny Schreiner declared that the property had become useless to her, since it was now home to the cemetery. She demanded restitution equal to the value of the property be made to her by the city of Plattling. According to a 25 February 1949 letter to the district administration office in Deggendorf, the mayor's office delegated the request "due to matters of jurisdiction" to the district administration of Deggendorf, objecting to the fact that the city had been expected to acquire the entire property of nearly 3,000 acres, even though the cemetery itself occupied less than an eighth of it. The district administration referred the mayor's office to a decree from 20 January 1947, stating that cemeteries for concentration camp victims were to be established and kept up by the communities themselves. Therefore, the state of Bavaria was responsible for the costs and an application would have to be submitted to the ministry of finance. They further requested that the owner of the property be asked whether she would agree to accept the amount 4,000 deutschmarks for the property. Fanny Schreiner declined, asking for 20,000 deutschmarks. In January 1950, a major consultation was scheduled for the case. According to information in the 14 January 1950 files of the Plattling City Council, Dr. Hoenig-Ohnsorg of the state restitution office suggested that exhumation would be the best solution in this matter. For the moment the Office of the Military Goverment for Germany and the United States, OMGUS, would probably not yet agree to such an idea, however, the question might very well "become acute" within a year. One month later the state restitution office and Fanny Schreiner signed a lease agreement for the part of the property occupied by the grounds of the cemetery. Paragraph 6 of the contract provided assigning the special status of historic or natural sanctuary to the rest of the property. This way it would be impossible, for as long as the cemetery remained located there, to make this property available for other building projects.

The Yearly Compulsory Exercise

On 30 August 1951, the *Isarbote* newspaper announced that there would be yet another memorial celebration at the concentration camp cemetery. They had been held regularly in the years immediately following the war, in 1946, 1947, and 1948; after that the interest in holding these services had begun to wane. The celebration in September 1951, in honor of the "Day of the Victims of Fascism," was the last one of its kind to take place. Beginning at 7:30 A.M., on 9 September 1951, celebratory services administered by the three dominant religious denominations, Protestants, Catholics, and Jews, had been planned. Wreaths were to be laid at the memorial. According to newspaper reports, "the comrades and delegations from Deggendorf were invited to be part of the memorial service in Plattling."

In September 1957, the remains of the former prisoners of the Plattling concentration camp were exhumed by members of the French tracing service and transferred to the concentration camp cemetery honoring the victims in Flossenbürg. Today, they lie in field C, rows 8a to 10c, bearing the individual grave numbers 1898 to 2084, the unofficial record of provisional disposal of a duty that had become onerous. The Plattling cemetery was dissolved without the public ever being aware of it. The obelisk was returned to the stonemasonry. According to statements by civilians, the material from the obelisk was used to manufacture other people's gravestones.

Decades Later—A New Beginning

It was 1985 when the deputy mayor of Plattling, Hermann Sterr, was sitting in a coffeehouse in the town of Offenbach, that he overheard a conversation at the neighboring table in which the name of his hometown was mentioned repeatedly. The people at the other table were speaking in English. Sterr became curious and joined the conversation. It was through this accidental encounter that he came to know the descendants of one Jewish family who had been expelled from Germany by the Nazis in the 1930s.

They exchanged addresses. Back home, Sterr immediately made an effort to establish contact with the local branch of the Jewish Cultural

Community, in the town of Straubing. In addition, during a town meeting he proposed that the once respected Jewish families of Plattling be officially honored. The mayor, Josef Kiefl, agreed and initially suggested a commemorative plaque as a way of honoring the families. According to the 11 September 1986 issues of the newspapers *Plattlinger Zeitung* and *Plattlinger Anzeiger*, the city council reached a unanimous decision to commission a commemorative plaque. Salomon Bronner, a member of the board of the Jewish Cultural Community of Straubing, and Deputy Mayor Sterr, agreed to cooperate on arranging the opening ceremony. Shortly thereafter, on 2 October 1986, the Jewish Cultural Community of Straubing wrote a letter to Mayor Josef Kiefl expressing astonishment at the plans, as "shortly after the war, a memorial in Plattling for the victims of the concentration camps had already been erected. This memorial" the letter continued "should still be in existence." Copies and photographs documenting the opening ceremony were included in the letter. The city administration's subsequent search for the whereabouts of the old obelisk, however, was in vain. And all that could be found in the city archives was an old yellowed poster and a newspaper report covering the celebration, which had taken place in 1946. This situation may have contributed to the ultimate decision to build yet another obelisk instead of installing the commemorative plaque.

The new memorial, an obelisk of greyish-blue Bavarian granite, is located at the entrance of the St. Jakob cemetery in Plattling. Engraved in Hebrew are the words: "IN MEMORY OF THE VICTIMS OF NATIONAL SOCIALISM AND THE JEWISH CITIZENS OF THE CITY OF PLATTLING, WHO HAD TO GIVE THEIR LIVES IN THE YEARS BETWEEN 1933 AND 1945." A short passage, in German, follows: "IN HONOR OF THE DEAD—A REMINDER TO THE LIVING." Both inscriptions are crowned by an engraving of the Star of David.

The Ceremony for the New Memorial

The new obelisk was unveiled and consecrated at 10 A.M. on 30 October 1987, in the presence of a large number of renowned and important guests. The event was covered by the newspapers, radio, and television. The next day, the *Plattlinger Anzeiger* newspaper reported: "It seems that the people of Plattling were finally, after forty years, awakened by a guilty conscience." At the beginning of the article Mayor Josef Kiefl was quoted in bold letters:

Especially in our town, where during the last months of the war the population directly witnessed the establishment of Plattling as the sub-camp of the Flossenbürg concentration camp, we must never forget the unspeakable suffering and the inhuman fate faced by those who were persecuted because of their religion, their race, and their worldview, and who, as a result, lost their homes, their freedom, and in many cases, their lives as well.

All this served as an opportunity, said Erich Spitz, spokesman of the Jewish Cultural Community, to commemorate all who drew the final breaths of their tortured lives without being guilty of any crime. "We remember the long-established family, Eugenie, Oskar, and Paul Kohn, and all the nameless victims who were members of the 'wrong' religion or held the 'wrong' worldview, and whose voices have now been silenced forever . . ."

CHAPTER 3

The Murdered Russians

In the final hours of the war, horrific massacres were committed in the Passau region against Russian prisoners of war. Scattered units of the Hitler Youth, the SS, the Volkssturm, and the Wehrmacht herded their emaciated victims into remote areas of nearby forests where they forced them to dig their own graves and then shot them in cold blood. Approximately 1,700 Russians lost their lives in this way. Except for a stone cross, hidden from sight beneath the thick in the undergrowth and forgotten, there is nothing left today to serve as a reminder of those crimes.

The Hacklberg Camp

In early March 1945, the Kreisobmann, or regional commander, of the German Workers Front (DAF), Herr Ratzesberger, informed the mayor of Passau that approximately 1,000 additional Russian POWs were expected to be arriving in Passau. The DAF decided that the brick factory belonging to the Episcopal Hacklberg brewery would serve as the new camp and made arrangements for the administration to occupy the quarters. Protests by Mayor Johann Fernberger did nothing to alter the decision. A few days later, a train filled with Russians arrived at the Donau Lände, a landing area along the Danube River in Passau. One of them, Nickolai Bestushov, recalled the events:

> I was born in 1912, in a village by the name of Jiernofka in Russia. They (the Germans) took me prisoner on 15 November 1941, in Machinsk. They held us there for a week, and then they took us to Poland, where I was put to work in a coal mine for one and a half years. When the Russian front began to close in, they took us and marched us to Passau, in Germany. The march lasted for two months. They held us there, in a camp, for one month. When we had left Poland, there were seven hundred of us. They shot many of the men who were weak; they also

shot the ones who asked for food. In the Passau camp we had to fill in all the bomb craters close to the camp, and when the railways were bombed, we had to work there for two days.

Anton Wallner, a farmer, was fifty years old at the time, and lived in Hacklberg. He gave the following statement regarding those times:

On 27 March 1945, about four hundred Russians were being held in the brick factory of Hacklberg, right next to my property. The commander was a lance corporal by the name of Gaida, who commanded another seventeen guard units, mostly consisting of older men. Gaida was later made leader of the camp. The first night the prisoners were put up in an open shed, with just a simple roof overhead. The shed was fenced in with wire, so that the prisoners could not get away. The next day I witnessed how the prisoners were beaten by the guards with sticks, because they had tried to get some food. But there was no food, because the food for the Russians at the camp came only ten days later. It was three days before the prisoners received their first food. It consisted of turnip soup and one slice of bread for the whole day. As the days passed I began to notice that a large part of the designated rations, such as animal fat and cigarettes, was set aside by the camp command, mostly by Gaida himself. The prisoners were aware of this, but there was nothing they could do about it. The Russians told us over and over again that all they were given was carrots, and that they knew nothing of any further rations.

Most of the remaining four hundred prisoners were put to work repairing the damage done to Passau's rail system; that meant, for the most part, clearing the rails of rubble and defusing and disposing of bombs, but also repairing the tracks themselves, as well as unloading rail cars.

Mayor Johann Fernberger of Hacklberg noticed that the Russians looked physically worn out. "Repeatedly the Russians had to carry back their fellow prisoners who had broken down at work." In 1950, Fernberger, in a self-congratulatory manner, told of how he had on one occasion given a load of firewood to the Russians, and on another occasion a cartload of turnips.

Fritz Stuis, leader of the Volkssturm in Passau, had been drafted to the army as an officer on 1 August 1939. Injured in 1944 in northern France, he came to the army hospital in Passau where Max Moosbauer contacted the Hauptmann of the reserve to take on the local Volkssturm. By he end of the year he was assigned to organize it, as kind of military expert. Even Stuis remarked: "Their condition was no longer normal."

Andreas Moser, a customs inspector from Passau who had been a first lieutenant and, since 1943, a control officer at the Landesschützenkompanie (regional rifle company—a division of the Wehrmacht), was responsible for accommodation, feeding, and work assignments at the camp. He worked for the DAF, and admitted that Russians were subject to stricter treatment because they could not be put to work individually, but needed to remain as a group, with an overseer, at all times. The 5th Company of the Landess-chützenbattalion (regional rifle battalion) number 5/515 had been trans-ferred from Silesia to guard the prisoners. By the end of March, the Volkssturm from the 4th Contingent (for the areas of Hacklberg, Hals, Grubweg, Heining, and Sandbach), which was commanded by the company leader and lawyer Ludwig Senninger, was forced to contribute an additional twenty men each day to stand guard from seven in the evening until five in the morning, in an attempt to provide extra security. On 24 May 1945, Lud-wig Senninger would be the first to provide a written statement about his involvement with the Volkssturm and these Soviets.

"Decent, Quiet, and Modest"

In exceptional cases, private individuals were able to "borrow" the Rus-sian prisoners. When attorney Senninger's house was badly damaged in a bombing raid on 19 March 1945, he rounded up ten prisoners to trans-port roof tiles. His wife, Elisabeth, who had never been a member of the Nazi Party or any of its organizations, knew the Russians were "harmless and industrious people." Because they were suffering from hunger she cooked potatoes for them and gave them two bowls of apples, for which they were apparently "very grateful." She described the Russians as "very decent, quiet, and modest." Still, their mistreatment continued. Anton Wallner reported in 1946:

> After bombing raids the Russians were set to work cleaning up the dam-age to houses of people who lived here in Hacklberg. As far as I remem-ber there were about ten Russians under the supervision of Johann Mins, who at the time was a member of the Volkssturm. I saw with my own two eyes how he used to hit them in their backs with the butt of his rifle, to make them work faster.

The Third Air Raid

At about 12:30 P.M., on 18 April 1945, twenty bomber squadrons approached Passau from the west, but then continued to fly east, crossing over the local Spitzberg, a hill just a block or so from the city center. At 1:55 P.M., approximately 120 bombers appeared over the city flying a north-south route. Without being intercepted by German air defense or flak, they proceeded to bombard the western part of the town. They dropped one delayed-action bomb, nearly seven hundred demolition bombs, as well as numerous incendiary bombs, of which twenty were duds. A few hours later the British Broadcast Service reported the attack, saying that the freight rail station had been bombed. The *Passauer Zeitung*, however, devoted not a single line to the incident. It only reported that the air raid sirens were still functioning normally, and on 23 April made a vague announcement about a memorial celebration for "the victims of an air raid."

Mass Murder at the Gas Works

Most of the damage from the air raids was done, indeed, to the rail system. Extremely hard work would be necessary to repair it. During one particular air raid by low-flying aircraft, the German guards literally pushed an army work commando made up of approximately two hundred Russians into the house at Bahnhof Strasse, number 9, which belonged to the barber Karl Kuchler. Karl Kuchler later stated that everything edible was stolen from the apartment. He further alleged that the Russians had broken the display window at the butcher shop of a Herr Bauer and stolen all the sausages. Eyewitnesses, however, reported that the window had been broken as a result of the detonation of the bombs. Kuchler, when asked specifically about the incident under oath on 28 August 1950, repeated that some two hundred Russian POWs had been chased into his entrance hall but he denied having seen any of them ripping apart live rabbits. He only had heard that from the railroad workers. About the subsequent murders he supposedly knew nothing. Landgerichtsrat Dr. Leiss, serving as investigating judge, listed his statement under transcript number 22/49, file AVZ 2 Js 3612/49. The fact remains, however, that soldiers of the Wehrmacht led the Russians from the work commando to the city gas works. Many of them were immediately shot and killed there by the SS. Today this location is the site of the Donaupassage—a local shopping mall. No memorial for the murdered Russian soldiers exists. During his interrogation Moosbauer stated to have heard about the executions at the Nikolakloster/Somme Barracks. But he denied any involvement.

In 1946, Anton Wallner stated the following in an official deposition:

I was told by a certain Herr Wiesner, who was a soldier then and has by now probably returned to his home town, that he took a group of forty Russian prisoners from the brick factory to the rail station immediately after the air raid on 18 April 1945. They were assigned to do repairs. Based on what Wiesner told me, seven Russians took the opportunity to loot the houses of civilians. Some of the Russians were found to have in their possession food, money, and some ration coupons. After that, Gaida himself shot and killed seven of the Russians. Their bodies were then taken to the cemetery.

Peter Plettl, who lived in the Kühberg area of Passau and who was employed at the German Rail at the time, stated the following in another deposition:

On 18 April 1945, I was walking home from work sometime in the afternoon. I was walking down the street behind the Stockbauer memorial vault toward the Kühberg; I stopped for a while when I saw four Russian prisoners coming out of the cemetery and throwing dead bodies into the ditch next to the wall at the corner of the Stockbauer memorial vault. I counted seven bodies. A guard asked me to keep an eye on the four Russians while he checked to see if indeed the three bodies had not been in the car with the others. The car he was talking about was from the factory in Passau-Hacklberg, where, according the guard, ten Russians had been shot and killed because of an alleged looting. It was clear, though, that others had already been buried next to the place where the bodies of the dead Russians were being tossed, as I saw some fresh graves there. This is all I know.

The police officer in training, Herr Huber, noted on 19 February 1946:

After having interrogated Plettl, I had him show me the place he was referring to and, on the same day, I notified the cemetery administrator, Herr Liebl. Herr Liebl informed me that he hadn't been out to the site yet as this was the first he had heard of it. I also pointed out to Herr Liebl another site, about eighty meters north of the wall, which appeared to be a mass grave. He will be taking further steps in the immediate future.

Murder at the Nikola Cloister

Another work commando of Russian forced laborers was being marched through the Ludwig Strasse in Passau when the air raid sirens went off.

While the guards ran toward the nearest bomb shelter, the Russians were left in the street to fend for themselves. They were left standing between the Hoft bakery and the Hotel Black Ox, whose owner was a well known member of the SS. They apparently took a few loaves of bread from the Hoft bakery, and some dumplings had gone missing from the pots of the hotel kitchen. The Russians were blamed. Nobody mentioned the fact that the premises where the Hoft bakery stood had, until shortly before the incident, been owned by Jews. The merchant Alfred Bernheim and his wife Berta had been expropriated by force and chased naked through the streets of Passau by the SA, until, penniless, they were "allowed" to emigrate to Palestine.

The Russian POWs were brought to the Somme Barracks, which today is the site of the Nikola Cloister and the University of Passau; they were shot there in the courtyard. The exact number of dead is not known. A granite memorial on the site commemorates the fallen German soldiers of the First World War. Nothing stands as a reminder of the murdered Russians. They were deemed criminals and have long been forgotten.

Paper Coffins

Retired editor in chief of the local newspaper, the *Passauer Neue Presse*, H. P. Heller, reported in 18 April 1985 issue that after the air raid in 1945 the transport capacities of the station had been one hundred percent compromised, as all of the tracks had been either blocked or destroyed. Heller also quoted the official government report, which stated under the heading of "UNUSUAL OCCURRENCES": "Shortly after the air raid Russian prisoners of war were caught red-handed removing food from a transport of wounded men that was stopped there. They were handed over to an SS pioneer garrison officer to be executed." Four Russians were shot on the spot by SS guards. The Passau railroad employee Johann Fröhler and others remember that the Russians were usually simply covered with dirt and not buried as required by law.

In a telegram dated 13 November 1941, it is stated that, "In cases where units of the Wehrmacht are required to bury deceased Russian POWs, the communities are responsible for immediate burial after the cause of death has been determined and officially certified by a coroner. The communities are free to decide for themselves whether . . . to arrange burials at existing cemeteries, or at other suitable sites." As it were, there was no provision for coffins. Instead the corpses were simply to be completely wrapped in heavyweight paper (if possible, paper fortified by oil, tar, or asphalt) or other suitable materials. The transport and burial is to be conducted discreetly. Multiple corpses should be interred side by side (and not one atop the other) in a common grave at a depth in accordance with local regulations. . . . In cases where it has been decided to bury the bodies in a cemetery . . . a remote section is to be chosen for the grave site. Celebrations or decoration of the graves are not permitted to take place. . . . Costs must be kept to the absolute minimum.

Corpses in the Bomb Crater

One night in April 1945, during the final days of the war, there was an incident in which Russian POWs were shot and simply thrown into a bomb crater. Johann Fröhler had observed this murder commando, and had heard the shots while working at the control tower. When he decided in the early morning hours to find out what had happened, he saw that one of the largest bomb craters in the area had just been freshly piled up with earth. He estimated that twenty to thirty prisoners had been buried there. In 1983 Fröhler bitterly related how since 1946 he had repeatedly reported what he had witnessed to the district attorney's office in Passau, but that his testimony was never recorded in a court of law.

Shortly after the war, Fröhler called on both district attorney Flossmann, as well as attorney general Loschelder, to exhume the Russians and identify them. Flossmann declined, Fröhler claims, because Loschelder allegedly had told him: "Flossmann, you will not do this. If you do, you'll have to deal with me!" In 1987, Fröhler turned to the Central Agency for Nazi War Crimes in Ludwigsburg. The agency contacted the department of public prosecution in Munich. An interrogation of Fröhler was arranged immediately. The result, however, has to date not been released. In 1946, Anton Wallner stated the following in a deposition:

> I know of about four to five Russians who are lying buried in the area of the brick factory, I do not know exactly where. I don't know how they died. I did not see it. Every day, a few Russians died; I am not sure of the illness they died from. I suspect it was the bad and scarce nutrition that was responsible. The Russians were usually taken to the graveyard around 1 P.M.

A letter dated 16 May 1942 proved that city councilman Bottler had received the instructions for the cemetery directly from Moosbauer, with the order to pass them on to the cemetery supervisor, Josef Heilmeier. The city archives filed this letter under the number II D 1/48 II B 3766. On 14 March 1943 an addendum regarding such deaths and transferable diseases followed. Herr Heilmeier stated the following on record:

> Near the wall outside of the graveyard twenty-four Russians are buried. These corpses were buried there by the Russians, in my absence. All I ever knew about them was their personal data, which I recorded. I cannot say whether these particular men died because they were shot or as a result of an illness. In addition to those twenty-four Russians, there are another six Russians buried at the cemetery, who died as a result of illness.

Police-officer-in-training Huber stated: "When I confronted him with the question of whether it was with full knowledge or as a result of his own stupidity or laziness that he apparently did not know what happened in his graveyard, despite being the warden of this cemetery, and if any other dead Allied soldiers were buried there," Heilmeier explained: "The dead were brought by the Wehrmacht and they were buried by prisoners. I could not tell you even if I wanted to whether there were any more Russians or people of any other nation buried there."

Simply Shot and Killed

The bomb damage sustained by the Moshammer bakery was so extensive that some of the Russians were called in to help with the repairs. To this day, Anna Würdinger remembers "those kind people." She explains:

> They did all the hard work, they lifted the flour vats and so on. They would always lend you a hand. We kept them around longer than they needed to perform the work, as they were so hungry. They always begged for food by pointing to their mouths! You know: "Hunger," "Bread," they used to say to us when the guards were not looking. Of course we gave them food. They liked the soup; it was warm, and they were freezing! Sometimes we shifted the potatoes from where they had been stored the day before so that the Russians could get another day's work out of it. One of them was an engineer, Sascha, and others, too —such noble people, and so young. And then, sometimes, when the guards used to steal bread from the bakery, that drove the Russians mad: "No stealing, you!" they would shout, before they would return the bread to us. Of course, later people might have said that it was the

Russians who had taken the bread. But none of them took anything from us. And then one day they were just taken away. They did not come any more. They were shot in the Neuburg forest. Just like that, without reason.

The Speech in Aicha v. Wald

Around 10 April 1945, county judicial president Dr. Spranger from Passau gave a speech before approximately 150 men and a few women in the Stauder Inn, in the town of Aicha v. Wald, some fifteen kilometers northeast of Passau. A poster announcing the event had been put up declaring that anybody who did not show up would be fined five reichsmarks. Years later an eyewitness recalled the speech. According to him, Dr. Spranger strongly declared the following: "As soon as the enemy arrives, all prisoners of war, enemies of the state, and traitors must be shot immediately." The entire assembly is said to have applauded enthusiastically. A few days after the meeting, writes Michael Gruber, almost one thousand men and women were murdered in a remote quarry.

Only Jakob Petri, the owner of a local mill, objected and told them that once the Americans had arrived they would be executed for these war crimes. It is rumored that Anna Gsottberger, the innkeeper, called the Passau district administration immediately afterwards saying that Petri was about to betray them all. On 28 April, Petri was murdered: he was shot through the neck by a member of the SS. Michael Gruber, who on 12 September 1948 had informed the district court in Munich about the murders in the quarry, was also found dead a short time later.

The Prisoners of the Passau Regional Rifle Company

Georg Lang, company leader of the Passau regional rifle company, whose battalion headquarters were located in the city of Straubing, confirmed in a hearing before the district attorney to have acted on "orders that the prisoners, with the exception of those prisoners committed to penal camps," were to be handed over to the mayors of the respective sites of deployment. The mayors then were to hand them over to the Americans. "His" rifle company, along with the prisoners of the penal camps, were ordered to "withdraw via Fürstenzell" and to "voluntarily" surrender to the Americans.

The "baby farm" in Sallach, at Gangkofener Strasse, number 7. Photo courtesy of the author.

Kazimiera Wronska (left) and her husband, Kazimier (center), were captured in the vicinity of Warsaw and deported to Germany to work as forced laborers. Photo courtesy of the author.

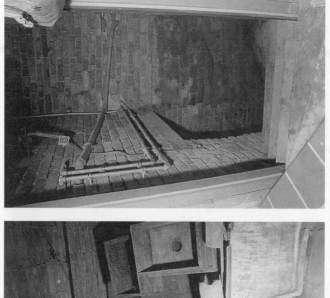

The entrance (left) to Barhof, number 3. The main building is where the murders of the infants and children took place. Stacks of children's coffins, and even piles of pacifiers, were found in the basement (center and right) at the end of the war. Photos courtesy of the author.

ABOVE AND OVERLEAF: Murders on the Inn Strasse: 748 Russians were
murdered here, many of them having been simply shot and tossed into the
Inn River. The exhumation site depicted is today the site of a children's
playground. Photos courtesy of the National Archives, Washington. D.C.,
111-SC-266700; 111-SC-266701; and 111-SC-266702.

The site in the Neuburg Forest where the murders of the Russians occurred is marked by a large memorial stone built in honor of a certain forest ranger by the name of Alois Ahr. There is no memorial to the Russian soldiers. Photo courtesy of the author.

The memorial to the murdered Russians, in Neumarkt in the Upper Palatinate region of Bavaria. The remains of the Russians were transferred here after the war. Photo courtesy of the author.

Lina Steidl witnessd the murders of twenty-five Russian officers in Neustift. Photo courtesy of the author.

The location of the murders in Neustift. Photo courtesy of the author.

The building in Oberjacking where some two hundred Russian POWs were held under miserable conditions. Photo courtesy of the author.

The barn in Tiefenbach where some two hundred Russians were rounded up and held until they were later executed. Photo courtesy of the author.

On this site in Kießling, ten Russian POWs were murdered by members of
the Hitler Youth. Photo courtesy of the author.

The platform at the Pocking train station as it appears today. In April of 1945, after a bombing raid had hit a train holding eight hundred concentration camp prisoners from the Buchenwald concentration camp killing many inside, the remaining prisoners, some fifty-six, were shot and killed for fear that they would escape. Photo courtesy of the author.

ABOVE AND BELOW: The Pocking memorial as it appears today. The inscriptions on the memorial, which included the names of the victims as well as the dates of their deaths and Stars of David, were all removed on an order from the State of Bavaria. Photo courtesy of the author.

DEN OPFERN DER
NATIONALSOZIALISTISCHEN
GEWALTHERRSCHAFT
1933–1945

Lang reports to have "simply set free" the French prisoners, asking only that they give their word of honor that they would not attack the local population. For the Russians and Poles, however, it was a different story: they began to march with the regional rifle company, as ordered, in the direction of Fürstenzell. It is unclear what happened to many of the prisoners. One fact, however, is certain: they were never handed over to the Americans. Neither did the rifle company surrender "voluntarily": Obersturmbannführer Krüger had ordered them to return to help defend Passau. The rifle company commanded by Captain Fuhrmann belonged to a different unit. More than half of the some 1,200 Russian prisoners under his command were apparently murdered.

The Struggle for Survival

Shortly before the arrival of the Americans, Captain Fuhrmann announced right out in the open to the mayor of Hacklberg, Herr Fernberger "that he was handing over to me the prisoners. I told him that I would not accept them." Such was Fernberger's testimony before the district attorney's office in 1950. Nickolai Bestushov remembered very clearly how in May 1945,

> When the Americans closed in, they [the Germans] took us away from where we were working; this was around noon on the third day—on 23 April 1945. We spent the rest of the day and the following night in the camp. On 25 April, at 3 P.M., the commander ordered those who were able to line up and those who were sick and could not march to remain where they were. Some 140 of us were well, and the 130 of us who were sick were left behind in Passau. Only 270 of us remained following the march from Poland. After that, the commander, who held the rank of a lieutenant, ordered 140 people to set off marching. Nobody knows where they took them. Before the lieutenant left he ordered four other soldiers to guard the sick and weak ones. On 25 April 1945 the 140 men set off.

Shortly thereafter Captain Fuhrmann informed the Passau district administrator, Dr. Zagel that he had had to leave behind 187 people who were unable to march. As a result, Dr. Zagel issued a written order stating that the surrounding communities of Hals, Grubweg, Salzweg, Thyrnau, Kellberg, Donauwetzdorf, Otterskirchen, and Kirchberg would be required to accept twenty men each and place them with the local farmers as laborers. The remaining twenty-seven were assigned to Hacklberg. On 26 April a document confirming this decision was already circulating. The document concluded with the words, "Any objections to the arrangement are to be refrained from, as there is no alternative."

It was not until 2 November 1950 that Dr. Friedrich Zagel was interrogated under oath. Landgerichtsrat Dr. Leiss served as investigating judge and listed his statement in transcript number 22/49, file AVZ 2 Js 3612/46. He admitted to having served as Landrat in Passau from February 1942 until 21 May 1945, but he claimed to have never heard about the shootings until being told by Mr. Kreipl. When confronted, however, with document number 162 from Moosbauer's de-Nazification file, he did finally admit to recognizing as his own the order to distribute the Russians; he added that he did not consider them any danger to the population, especially since most of them were sick.

Mass Murder in the Neuburg Forest

In the early dawn of 26 April 1945, a massacre that was to last three full days began to unfold at the southern border of Passau. Russian POWs from the neighboring communities of the Passau region were led in the direction of Fürstenzell and brutally murdered in the Neuburg Forest. Today this location is the site of a childrens' playground. On 16 May 1945, a secretary from Passau named Fanny Holzer testified under oath before Captain Fred W. Hofstetter, the American officer in charge of investigations, and the court-certified translator, Therese Baumgärtler. In what would later be filed by the U.S. authorities under exhibit 8, Ms. Holzer stated:

> On 26 April 1945, we drove into the Neuburg Forest at about 4 A.M. and arrived in Apfelkoch at about 5:30 A.M. Once we arrived there we thought that we were hearing the sounds of low-flying airplanes; that's how close the shooting was. We fled, trying to hide in garages, looking for cover. Then we were told not to worry and that we could proceed into the forest, that the shooting would not harm us. At the edge of the forest we were told by a member of the SS to stop. We saw, to the right of the path, about five meters away from us, five or six dead or dying Russians. One of them tried to raise himself up. He looked at us as though he expected us to help him. To the right side there were even more dead bodies—about ten or twelve of them I would estimate. The SS man walked over to us, and when he saw how horrified we were . . . he said, "You should be glad that you're rid of the Russians, they're troublemakers and thieves. Three of them escaped during the transfer

and we're still looking for them. Maybe they went into the water and drowned, or maybe they swam across."

Maria Barmbichler, who was a fourteen-year-old student at the time, testified on 16 May 1945, in what would later be filed as exhibit 13:

> On 26 April 1945, at 5:30 A.M. we heard shots being fired in the Neuburg Forest. We thought that they were low-flying airplanes and wanted to get to the forest as quickly as possible. There were a couple of heavily armed SS men standing nearby. We walked a few steps further and that's when I saw the dead men lying on the left side of the street; they were wearing gray-green uniforms. One lifted his head a little and looked at us with his eyes wide open. I don't know how many there were, because I looked away immediately. We continued to hear shots.

Fanny Dirschl, a bank employee, contributed the following statement in her sworn testimony taken on 16 May 1945 and later filed under exhibit 7:

> As I looked closer at the scene around me, I saw several Russians who had already been shot, but who were not yet dead, lying in the grass on the left side of the street; further back there were two more Russians who seemed to be dead already. Several more were lying on the right side of the street; I cannot remember how many exactly, because I was terrified. When I asked the SS soldier if they [the SS] had been the ones doing the shooting, he answered: "Yes, and you should be happy to be rid of these Russians; they were caught stealing, and they even broke into one woman's home." They were supposed to be transferred to another camp. Then the SS soldiers told us to move on, that this was not something women should see.

Maria Mohr was yet another who saw three members of the SS and the dead Russians. In her testimony taken on 16 May 1945, in what would later be filed as exhibit 10, she stated: "I was so shocked and confused when I saw them, I can't remember exactly how many there were. One of the SS men told us: 'get moving and be glad the Russians are gone.'" Fanny Holzer recalled further:

> The shooting continued. We were allowed to walk on a little farther and there we saw something moving; the others saw more Russians there. I couldn't really tell myself, but I saw an SS man going in that direction; only when a second SS man arrived did we ask if we could continue on

our way. He didn't answer us at all. I gave this testimony in writing on 16 May 1945, and I swear that I've told the truth, so help me God.

Maria Mohr elaborated:

> Several meters further on, at the edge of the forest, an SS lieutenant yelled out: "Halt!" There was a bend in the path ahead of us and from there we heard more gunshots and more orders being shouted out. I couldn't understand what they were saying, because I'm hard of hearing. But I realized that something terrible was happening. I couldn't make out any details, because the area where the shooting was taking place was hidden from sight. An SS lieutenant said: "Three Russians escaped during transport to Schärding. They are either somewhere in the forest or they waded into the water." I did not believe their explanation, however.

Maria Barmbichler noticed the following: "I saw the Russians crouching low under some trees. Two of the Russians had shovels. I couldn't see anything else except that one of the poor Russians was making the sign of the cross." Hans Georg Mohr, who was a fourteen-year-old apprentice at the time, stated in his testimony from 16 May 1945, in what would later be filed as exhibit 11: "I saw one of them struggling to stay alive. I recognized one of the SS lieutenants and an SS Sturmmann from the insignias on their uniforms. Therese Baumgärtler also saw "five or six dead Russians" as well as "a group of men who were kneeling over by the edge of the forest" when more shots were being fired. "I did not see how they were taken away, all I remember was that two men in gray soldiers' overcoats were sent up the hill with shovels in their hands." Fanny Dirschl added: "We had to remain standing there until the group of Russians was chased further into the forest amid much screaming and shouting. Afterwards all you heard was shooting." Therese Klein, too, recalled the shocking experience, and she neither could forget the "terrifying images." She stated in her testimony from 16 May 1945, in what would later be filed as exhibit 9: "We were not allowed to continue any further until these poor people were carried off deeper into the forest. The SS soldier explained to us, without our even having asked a single question, that these Russians had stolen some jewelry."

On 18 July 1950, Landgerichtsrat Dr. Leiss interrogated Max Hidringer under oath. His statement is listed as transcript number 22/49, file AVZ 2 Js 3612/46. In it Max Hidringer recalled:

On the early morning of 26 April 1945, I was riding my bicycle from Vornbach back to Passau, on the street that ran along the Inn River. While passing through the Neuburg Forest I was told by several people I encountered along the way coming from the opposite direction that there was combat taking place in the forest. They couldn't tell me whether it involved American or Russian troops. Since I was in a hurry I did not even get off my bike, but instead kept on pedaling. When I got to the end of the forest I ran into three SS guards. They didn't say anything to me and I didn't say anything to them. After I had pedaled up a small incline some one hundred meters away, I ran into another SS guard; two Russian prisoners were standing next to him. On the meadow that separates the Inn River from the adjacent street, various pieces of equipment, such as bags for rations, were found, typical of the type the Russians carried. In the street itself I saw large pools of blood, which were obviously quite fresh. It immediately occurred to me that a group of Russian prisoners had just been murdered there. I felt terribly sorry for the two Russian prisoners I had seen standing next to the SS man, because I knew that first they would be made to clean up and then they would be taken out and shot as well.

Later it was reported in the *PNP:* "The screams of the Russians who were thrown into the Inn River while still alive were heard throughout the surrounding area." At that point, most of the bodies had been buried. Still, uniformed soldiers carried large numbers of Russian army overcoats down to the Inn and threw them into the river. The goldsmith August Hell and his sister Berta were traveling at the time together with the architect A. Dölger, who was accompanied by his wife and son, in the direction of the Neuburg Forest. As soon as they arrived at the Maierhof Barracks they heard a series of shots being fired. Berta Hell, a secretary at the Passau diocesan youth care center, testified on 16 September 1945, in what would later be filed under exhibit 6: "A short distance before the spot where the large cross stands beside the road I encountered a woman on her bicycle who was completely terrified. She said: 'They're shooting Russians over there.'"

At the Hoffmann nursery they finally encountered a group of at least thirty people. Among them August Hell recognized Theo Bottler and his brother, as well as the coal dealer Karl Resch. Hell testified before the CIC in 1945. But it was not until 19 July 1951 that Hell's interrogation by Landgerichtsrat Dr. Leiss, who served as the investigating judge, would be listed his statement in transcript number 22/1949, file AVZ 2 Js 3612/46 as well. On the same day, Karl Resch was also interrogated by

Landgerichtsrat Dr. Leiss. He claimed to neither have seen any of it nor to remember anything.

Berta Hell, however, remembers the incident very well:

> When I arrived at the Hoffmann nursery I saw the Nazi government official Theo Bottler and his brother, the train conductor Herr Bottler; they were walking toward the city. My brother, August Hell, who accompanied me, said: "No doubt those pigs were there to watch the Russians be murdered." On a meadow to the left of the street, on the banks of the Inn River, we saw a couple of SS men standing there, and several others were occupied over by an embankment. There were some large bundles lying in the grass, which looked like piles of clothing. The meadow appeared to be entirely trampled over and there were traces of the kind made by dragging heavy objects. We assumed that they were the result of dragging dead bodies across the grass and over to the Inn River where they were thrown in. We no longer saw any bodies, but there was blood in the street. This must have been close to 8 A.M.

Johann Auer, who was preparing to open his barn to shelter refugees, stated in his 16 May 1945 testimony, in what would later be filed as exhibit 5, that he had discovered traces of the massacre in his meadow, at Inn Strasse, number 92. All matter of equipment and clothing were found floating on the Inn River, as well as many dead bodies. During the day all was quiet, most likely in order not to cause any further disquiet to the population living close by. But the murders continued: on the morning of 26 April, a member of the Volkssturm who was ordered to serve the night shift reported that the regional rifle company number 5/515 and their captain had left for Eholfing near Sulzbach. The 293 prisoners had rations for only a single day.

Ludwig Senninger claimed that only three members of the rifle company were left to guard the prisoners, and allegedly Russians had stolen "numerous" hens and other provisions. Inquiries at the brick factory in Hacklberg allegedly confirmed that approximately sixty Russian POWs had been unable to march. The plan by the Passau district administrator to farm out the Russians to various neighboring communities would have hardly been feasible, according to Mayor Fernberger, as this would have involved hour-long marches.

The Front Approaches

After the Russian troops had taken over the towns of Mährisch-Ostrau and Troppau the 53rd Soviet Army took the town of Brünn on 26 April

1945. The 5th U.S. Army had now reached Verona and the 2nd British Army had reached Bremen. The reports of the Wehrmacht read: "Fighting ensued in the Bavarian Forest in the area of Zwiesel." The city of Regensburg was surrounded, and the towns of Kötzing and Freyung v. Wald were already occupied. The 26th U.S. Infantry Division had pushed ahead via Bogen toward Deggendorf, and the city of Plattling was under artillery fire. In Passau, tank barricades were set up along the streets leading toward the Neuburg Forest. At the edge of the forest adjacent to Neuburg Street medium artillery were set up and fired toward Tiefenbach. A battery set up in what is today Breslauer Strasse was firing off into the same direction. The Americans, however, had nearly reached Waldkirchen. No defensive positions were set up there and there were no German troops present; local party leaders called for help from Austria: SS units were already on their way in order to stop the American advance.

Spare Me Your False Sentimentality

The lawyer Ludwig Senninger demanded reinforcement for the guard posts. That same morning he discussed the situation with Captain Stuis and Major Eichhorn at the quarters of the district staff leadership of the Volkssturm in Ludwig Strasse, number 13. Stuis and Senninger then met with the mayor and district leader of the NSDAP, Herr Moosbauer. In opposition to district administrator Dr. Zagel, Moosbauer was of the opinion that the distribution of prisoners among the local farmers would pose the "greatest possible danger to the local population" and intended to see to it that Captain Fuhrmann would be punished. Senninger quoted the mayor further: The Russians were to be sent to the Neuburg Forest under the pretense of having to do some ditch digging, and "if there was no other way they would have to be killed off." During his de-Nazification trial (on page five of his interrogation, and page 177 of the final file) Moosbauer admitted to having said that he did not care what should come of the Russians, even if they should ultimately be killed. When Captain Stuis resolutely objected to this, Moosbauer is said to have answered: "Spare me your false sentimentality. This is war!" Upon their return, Senninger informed mayor Fernberger and the district administrator that the Russians would have to remain in the camp until further notice. That same evening he was ordered to appear at the offices of the Volkssturm: Fuhrmann had been summoned back and promised to take the prisoners to Sulzbach the next morning. Transportation would be provided for the very sick. On 22 October 1947 Stuis would be interrogated about

Fuhrmann's sudden departure and return from the Rottal (case file 6031/ St. See also the denazification protocol from 12 January 1948, case file 234/ R 27138/A 6013).

Senninger was not yet at home when the SS Sturmführer Erhard Thoma attempted to pay him a visit. Elisabeth Senninger asked him into the kitchen. Thoma told her that all of the Russians would be shot. The execution commando was already waiting in the street. When Senninger came home he informed Thoma that the problem had just been resolved: the Russians would not be shot, but instead were to be taken away by the regional rifle company. Thoma seemed relieved and said that he would be returning immediately to the Somme Barracks. On 24 October 1946 Elisabeth Senninger, nee Müller, would sign under oath a four page statement about that scene and the Soviet POWs.

The Murders Continued at Night

As early as 4 P.M., Anna Dupper, who lived at Inn Strasse, number 100, testified during an interrogation at her home on 4 March 1949, that she saw sixty Russians enter the Neuburg Forest accompanied by two soldiers. Several hundred Russians followed in smaller groups. Johann Auer, a fifty-eight-year-old gardener and farmer who lived at Apfelkoch Strasse, number 12, made the following declaration:

> At about 8 P.M. I saw three to four groups of Russians and German soldiers march past my house. There were about thirty Russians in each group. . . . Six to eight guards were assigned to each group, each with a rifle over his shoulder; I think they were SS men. The shooting lasted until six in the morning. My wife heard the shooting as well and we talked about it later. . . . Two days later I was walking across a meadow on my property, close to Maria Robl's house. This particular piece of land leads up from the street all the way down to the river and is located about one hundred meters from the crossroads. I saw that the grass was all trampled; there were several pools of blood, some of them fresh. One trail of blood led all the way down to the Inn River; the corpses were most likely dragged along there. There were Russian army caps lying scattered on the grass. Five days later I returned to mow the grass because my cows would not eat it.

Up until 8 or 9 P.M. Johann Auer, who was interrogaed at his home on 4 March 1949, testified that he saw five groups of about thirty men each, all accompanied by armed Wehrmacht soldiers. During questioning, Maria

Robl testified under oath: "On the night of 26 April I saw 130 Russians walking down Apfelkoch Strasse, number 24—it was about 10 P.M. There were fifteen SS men from the Somme Barracks with them. They accompanied the Russians as they walked through the streets. The groups turned left at our house."

Adam Holowetzki from Czernowitz recalled: "On the evening of 26 April I saw a group of 130 men as they took a break around 10 P.M. on Apfelkoch Strasse. There also were 15 to 20 SS men from the Somme Barracks in Passau. It was the guards who were accompanying the Russians, who had also stopped and were sitting in the Apfelkoch Strasse. They then sat down in front of our house." He continued: "Starting at 2 A.M. on 27 April I heard the shooting in the Neuburg Forest. I heard machine guns and carbines until 6 A.M., and I did not see anybody return from the forest." Maria Robl confirmed this: "From 2 A.M. until 6 A.M. on 27 April I heard the fire of machine guns and carbines. I did not see any of the Russians return from the forest. At 6 A.M. I saw a group of fifteen Russians kneeling down at the edge of the forest; they were eating grass; an SS man was standing in front of them. The men were equipped with shovels." On 9 August 1950, when Landgerichtsrat Dr. Leiss interrogated Robl under oath in what would later be filed under transcript number 22/49, file AVZ 2 Js 3612/46, she added that Johann Auer had told her mother that that afternoon Mr. Bottler had warned him not to enter the forest. Ludwig Robl, who lived at Inn Strasse, number 102, and witnessed 120 Russians being shot and then buried in the forest approximately three hundred meters from his property, also saw about twenty-four other Russians kneeling on the Dupper meadow; the following day they were crying and praying. After they were forced to bury their comrades and eradicate as much as possible any traces of the crime, they, too, were shot. Maria Robl added: "We also saw at the edge of the Neuburg Forest, on the spot where there is a wooden bench today, approximately fifteen to thirty Russians kneeling, crying, and praying. They were holding shovels and an SS man was standing behind them with a loaded rifle. These Russian POWs were then shot out on the field that was leased by Herr Auer, between the Inn River and the street."

The Lipka Commando

On 17 May, with the help of interpreter Corporal Joseph Sobolesky, Nicholai Bestushov, from the village Jiernofka in Russia, was sworn in in

Neuburg. Thereupon, Sobolesky states in his written deposition, "due to the fact that the said Nicholai Bestushov was unable to write, he dictated the foregoing statement to me in the Russian language and that the above statement was read back to him by me in the Russian language before he subscribed in his own handwriting in my presence." The document would become exhibit 4. Bestushov states how "the four soldiers gave orders that the 130 of us who were sick were to get up and get ready to go to the hospital. Those who couldn't walk at all were put on trucks. When all of us were ready to march we saw another 170 men who were sick, coming down the street. They took these 170 men and put them together with us, so that altogether we were about 300 men." Exhibits 2, 3, 4, 14, 14a, and 15 all confirm the column of some three hundred prisoners guarded by some thirty SS soldiers from the Somme Barracks. The files of the Passau district attorney's office reveal the following: on the morning of 27 April Sergeant Lipka arrived with a transfer commando; at 11:10 A.M. he signed a document confirming that he had taken over the command of 289 Russian prisoners of war. The POWs were "subsequently taken away in several groups." Exhibits 2, 3, and 4 corroborate this fact.

Exhibits 2 and 3 further corroborate what the locals saw and heard. The killings would last four hours. Nickolai Bestushov's group's turn came relatively late. In May 1945 he dictated the following declaration in Russian (translated into English by Captain Joseph Sabolesky), and declared before God to its truth:

> On 28 April 1945, at 1 A.M., the new officer, along with thirty other new people, gave us orders to get moving. This is when we became aware that we were not really being transported to any hospital after we saw some thirty guards arriving with shovels. They had us march along the road leading to the Inn River and then they made us stop in a clearing on the edge of the Neuburg Forest. We were all ordered to lie down flat on the ground. Then the officer, accompanied by fifteen of the guards, went into the Neuburg Forest. The remaining fifteen guards told us to stay where we were and ordered us not to move, or else we would be shot right then and there. The officer and the other fifteen guards then returned from the forest to where we lay. They counted out ten men and had them stand up. Then they led those ten men into the forest. About ten minutes passed and then we heard shots. After that they came back and took ten more men with them. About fifteen minutes later we heard more shots. They continued leading men off in groups of ten into the forest until there were only about forty of us left. A few of us

whispered to each other that we might as well try to escape. It was almost morning when two women walked by pulling a little cart in the direction of Passau. I got up with a few others and we started to run toward to forest. I could hear the shots whistling right past my ears. When I reached the forest I ran into another friend and we continued running deeper into the forest where we sat down and rested for a while. We were hiding in that forest for one day and one night. We began to get hungry, and around midday I told my friend, let's go back to where we fled from and see if we can find our things and maybe something to eat. We went back to the field from where we had escaped and saw that there was nobody there; the field had been mowed. There was blood in some places, but most of the ground had been cleaned up and we saw traces of blood leading down to the Inn River, so we knew that the men who were shot in that field were thrown into the river. We looked around and began to fear that somebody might see us. We were growing even hungrier and then it started to rain. We went to a nearby house and were given something to eat.

Maria Robl, too, was looking for traces of the crimes. On 28 or 29 April Anna Dupper discovered two escaped Russians among the Poles, Hungarians, and Romanians who were being sheltered in her barn. Initially they were made to stand outside her house against a tree; in the evening a car with SS officers drove up and took the two into the forest.

Eyewitnesses, as well as the *PNP* reported later, in converging testimonies, that the majority of the Russians had been shot at the Herrgottsbauer and had been hastily covered with soil in the embankment and in a small cave where today a children's playground is located. The cave can today no longer be found. It is not clear if it was in fact filled with bodies and then intentionally filled in. Others were killed at a rock on the banks of the Inn River and then pushed into the water.

Max Hidringer recalls:

On Sunday, 29 April 1945, I rode my bicycle along the Inn River from Passau to Vornbach, as usual. When I got to the large outdoor crucifix in Apfelkoch I was stopped by an officer of the Wehrmacht who had with him several other soldiers. When I returned from Vornbach to Passau that same evening I ran into another Wehrmacht guard in the same place. Two Russian POWs, who looked very bad, were lying close to the embankment of the river. I thought to myself that these Russians would probably be shot as well that evening. But I did not ask any questions. I don't know if they actually were shot. These guards were not SS soldiers, they were members of the Wehrmacht.

Finally the massacre ended. Maria Robl told how she

> . . . discovered a Russian prisoner in the air raid shelter close to our
> house, who had been wounded on his foot and had escaped the killings
> by pretending to be dead. He then told us that he had been hastily
> buried alive along with his dead comrades, and that he had dug himself
> out and crawled to our shelter after the SS had left. We gave him milk
> and bread and then he hid again, as he was still afraid of the SS. . . . A
> flight captain from Munich who later had coffee with us told us that the
> SS had shot the Russians. He himself had been ordered to participate in
> the action, but he had kept himself in the background and had not shot
> any Russians himself.

Nickolai Bestushov, one of the massacre's few survivors, testified further:
"I don't know for certain if these guards were from the SS or not. . . . All
the men who were murdered that night by the guards were Russian
POWs; I don't know any other reason for why they were murdered except
for that they were Russian and prisoners of war. I only know the names of
two of them. . . . Ivan Siechenko and Alexander Chernov." Maria Robl
could not erase the memory of the Russians from her mind. She searched
for traces of the crime and testified a short time later:

> In the forest, from the place where the shooting came, I found three
> graves filled with dead Russians. Three days later Hans Auer told me
> that the Russians had been shot in his field right next to the street. I
> went there and saw that there was a strip about one meter wide leading
> from the field to the river; the clothing of the dead Russians was lying
> in the bushes, close to the river. The three graves we saw must have held
> about twenty to thirty men total—the graves were loosely covered with
> soil and leaves.

Survival by Chance

On the morning of 1 May 1945, Ludwig Senninger was informed that
Sergeant Lipka had not received permission to use any vehicles for trans-
porting some sixty prisoners who were unable to walk, and that he had left
them in the company of three guards. The prisoners were ultimately left
unattended during the entire four days. In an attempt to alleviate the
worst of the misery, Dr. Zagel supplied two hundred pounds of flour from
Gaißamühle that had originally been intended for refugees. Allegedly the
mayor approved of an additional cart of potatoes. In the meantime forty

more Russians had joined the group. Most likely these were Russians who had been able to flee from other camps and work commandos. Ludwig Senninger testified that he had informed Mayor Fernberger in writing of his intention to confiscate the eight to ten hundredweights of potatoes from the cellar of a local brewery and to make them available to the Russians, unless he (Fernberger) did not agree by 4 P.M. to guarantee food supplies for the one hundred prisoners. Upon this, Fernberger went to the Americans, who were stationed in Patriching and who then came with trucks and picked up the Russians on the morning of 2 May. The war in Passau had come to an end; the city was about to be officially signed over to the Americans.

Bodies Found

Immediately after the end of the war, Rudolf von Scholtz, who was appointed as the new mayor of Passau by the Americans, found several dead bodies and showed the Americans the location of his discovery. On 13 May 1945, Edward R. Garrison, the Deputy Director at the Office of Military Government in Passau turned to him, in reference to their "recent conversation concerning the moving of thirty-five Russian bodies, buried in a shallow mass-grave in the outskirts of Passau." On 16 May, Captain Fred W. Hofstetter ordered inquests to be conducted by the 3rd U.S. Army in order to come to some reliable conclusions in the matter. Captain Harold S. Sandhaus was assigned to the exhumation as a medical expert and on 17 May 1945, gave the following report on 16 May 1945, which would later be filed under exhibit number 16:

> The bodies had been deposited into two ordinary graves. They were laid down into a hollow in the earth and the bodies were covered with a thin layer of soil. The corpses were in various stages of decay, depending on their depth of immersion into the earth; my guess is that they had been dead anywhere from thirteen to eighteen days. The corpses were fully clothed and pieces of equipment such as eating utensils and other items were still present. The abbreviation S.U. was visible on the coats and sometimes the pants of the dead. When examining the bodies I immediately recognized that many of the dead had gunshot wounds to their heads. The entrance wound was small, while the exit wound was extremely large. It was difficult to determine the kind of weapon that would have inflicted this kind of injury. Others had wounds that were evidently caused by a rifle, which had shattered the skull. As I examined

the 107 exhumed bodies I was struck by the fact that almost none of the wounds were located on the lower half of the body—that is to say nowhere below the neck. All in all I saw two burial locations; there were 116 bodies in the first one, and 91 bodies in the second one. The trees in the immediate neighborhood of the site revealed scarring that may have been a result of the bullets. In my estimation the obvious cause of death in the 107 exhumed corpses is physical violence.

After the inquest Major Gart of the war crimes team in Regensburg had no objections to their reburial. He recommended they proceed as soon as possible. However, he requested that should "any further evidence in the form of actual witnesses to these death" be uncovered, that he be notified. The Americans ordered former Passau Nazis to exhume the bodies. All the citizens of Passau between sixteen and sixty years of age were ordered to watch while the bodies were buried in the Russian cemetery across from the city hospital.

For the Record

On 17 May 1945, Friedrich Pusch testified under oath before the American officer Dwight McKay. With the assistance of interpreter Sgt Athmar Betz, Pusch was sworn in. In exhibit 17 we read:

From 1935 until 1938 I was a member of the Austrian Legion in Germany. The Austrian Legion was part of the NSDAP. In 1938 I returned to Germany. In Austria I had established the Pioneer units of the General SS (1st Battalion). From 1 January 1940 until 6 March 1941, I served as company leader of the training and reserve battalion number 1 in Dresden; from 7 March 1941 until 7 March 1943, I was Pioneer unit instructor at the Junkerschule in Bad Tölz. From 2 March 1943 until 29 April 1943, I was commander of the Pioneer school in Hrondis-chko (Czechoslovakia). From 25 August 1943 until 25 August 1943, I was commander of the Pioneer training battalion in Passau. The Pioneer training battalion number 2 was stationed partly at the Somme Barracks and partly at the Maierhof Barracks. Captain Schüssler, Obersturmführer Lange, Untersturmführer Herrmann, Obersturmführer de Vries, as well as Untersturmführers Brodmann, Sandner, Wolff, Zinn, and Kreische, were officers at the Somme Barracks. There were also other officers of the Wehrmacht stationed at the Somme Barracks. I personally know Stabsintendant Stegermeier. . . . The testimony of Stm. Gutsch seems credible in my estimation; today is the first that I have heard of any Russian soldiers that were shot.

On 2 July 1945, Captain Howard D. E. Noyd of the 12th U.S. Army, who also was a member of the War Crimes Branch, compiled the following summary:

> On 25 April 1945, Colonel Becher was responsible for all POW camps in the vicinity of Passau and Obersturmbannführer Friedrich Pusch commanded all the SS troops stationed at the Somme Barracks, which included the pioneer battalion; Stabsintendant Stegermeier was his aid. Untersturmführer Kreische was company leader of the 1st training company of the Second Pioneer Battalion. Other SS officers who were stationed at the Somme Barracks included Obersturmführer Lange, Untersturmführer Herrmann, Obersturmführer De Vries, Untersturmführer Zinn. Obersturmführer Lange was legal officer at the Somme Barracks and thus authorized to give orders for the execution of prisoners. Lange received his orders from the SS and from the police courts in Bayreuth and Bamberg.

The assessment by Howard D. E. Noyd reads as follows: "The inquest findings are satisfactory and any further inquests have not been ordered. Obvious war crimes have been identified and provisions have been made to try and apprehend the perpetrators. Wanted persons lists for all aforementioned individuals have been recorded in the files at the headquarters of the 3rd Army." In addition, in July 1945 Colonel C. E. Mickelwait requested permission from the headquarters of the First French Army to access information about Karl Stegmaier, whose name was also mentioned in connection with the Dachau trial, as there was a possibility that he could be the same as Stabsintendant Stegermeier. On 16 April 1947, Colonel C. E. Straight wrote to the director of the authorities in charge: "Herewith this headquarters is sending you information in connection with the murder of approximately 660 Russians at the end of April 1945, in Passau, Germany. This information is being forwarded to the Russian authorities."

It was not possible, however, to determine exact numbers, as neither the city nor the district administration office in Passau had any "documents or other proof." Only verbal records existed concerning POW commandos, and "the names were, for the most part, unknown." This, at least, was the conclusion arrived at by the Passau District Administrator Karl, on 5 December 1953.

The Only Judges Left Were Old Nazis

A letter written by the Passau senior public prosecutor, dated 11 May 1948, states:

The murder of prisoners of war is a crime against human rights, against humanity, and against common morality, a crime of such gravity that it can never be justified as a simple matter of internal national law or of simply following official orders, as to ever be categorized as a justified act. It thus follows that anyone, even during the Nazi era, who ever participated knowingly in such a crime effectively fulfilled the objective criteria for qualifying as either a crime against humanity or of his having participated in murder. . . . When faced with the gravity of such a crime the perpetrators will not be permitted to invoke the notion that Nazi law not only did not declare such acts as subject to punishment, but that in some cases it even ordered them to be committed; it follows that the claim of ignorance at having broken a law cannot apply in the case of a violation against a common law of morality of this kind of gravity.

Investigations, however, began relatively late, as a reliable legal system simply did not exist in Passau until 1949. Indeed the overwhelming majority of the remaining legal professionals were not permitted to practice because of their Nazi past. Here and there a state superior judge from Munich traveled there to conduct some business, but he had to take the train back that same evening because there was simply no room to be found to stay overnight in Passau. On 12 July 1950, Landgerichtsrat Dr. Leiss finally interrogated Karl Probst, listing his statement as transcript number 22/49, file AVZ 2 Js 3612/46. Probst stated that he had been a local officer in the Wehrmacht, holding the rank of captain. Becher's adjutant was August Muggenthaler from Straubing.

On 6 November 1950, August Muggenthaler was interrogated under oath. Landgerichtsrat Dr. Leiss served as investigating judge and listed his statement under transcript number 22/49, file AVZ 2 Js 3612/46. August Muggenthaler made the following statement in 1950:

From February 1945 up until the collapse [of the Third Reich] I was active captain and assistant to Colonel Becher, specifically in his role as commander of the local army district. I served exclusively at the local commando. The commando was set up in the Maierhof Barracks. As the one with seniority in that particular location, Colonel Becher also had an office at the Nikolai Barracks. He also had an aid serving him there. I do not recall the name of this officer. During my time he was the senior officer in that location, and in this capacity, he had command over all of the troops of this particular area. However, I myself had nothing do to with the SS or with the tactical assignments of Colonel Becher. With the approach of the Americans the hierarchy of order deteriorated increasingly as a result of the confusing arrival of deserting troops, and so I cannot really provide any reliable information as to who actually held the highest military authority in Passau during those final days.

On 7 August 1950 Andreas Straßburger was interrogated under oath. Landgerichtsrat Dr. Leiss served as investigating judge and listed his statement in transcript number 22/49, file AVZ 2 Js 3612/46. Straßburger was able to give more precise information in 1950:

> On 21 April 1945 I came to Passau as a lieutenant colonel. I was assigned to be the liaison officer. When I arrived in Passau, Colonel Becher was the commander in charge of combat. This officer was killed in action during the assault on Passau. After him—I don't remember if it happened before his death or shortly after—SS Obersturmführer Pusch became commander in charge of combat. Pusch's staff included a Hauptsturmführer Schiessl or Schüssler and an Untersturmführer Herrmann, the latter being an assistant. Pusch and Schüssler once drove by car together to Hutthurm and during this trip they crashed and later died. Afterwards Herrmann took over business affairs for the commander for about a day. After him a Wehrmacht colonel became commander in charge of combat. He remained in this position until the American approach.

On 7 August 1950 Andreas Moser was interrogated under oath. Landgerichtsrat Dr. Leiss served as investigating judge and listed his statement under transcript number 22/49, file AVZ 2 Js 3612/46. Andreas Moser made the following comments regarding the general situation of the POWs:

> From 1943 I was lieutenant colonel and control officer with the regional rifle company for the district of Passau. Captain Georg Lang, from the city of Amberg, was the company leader. The battalion staff was stationed in Straubing. I do not recall the battalion number. As control officer it was my task to supervise the POWs who were assigned in my area. I was responsible for accommodations, food, work assignments, etc. There also were some Russians among the POWs, who received a stricter treatment, which is to say they were not to be used for individual labor assignments. There did not exist any orders to treat them any worse, to abuse them, or even kill them. Violence was only officially permitted at the Büchlberg POW penal camp, to be used on those who refused to work.

Shortly before the Americans arrived we received orders to transfer the POWs, with exception of those in the penal camps, into the jurisdiction of the mayor of the respective assignment areas; the mayors were then to hand them over to the Americans. The regional rifle company itself was to retreat with the POWs from the penal camps in the direction of Fürstenzell and to then voluntarily surrender with their prisoners to the Americans. In clear violation of these orders, I did not take with me a group of French POWs during this disengagement movement; instead I sent them back toward Hauzenberg after I had received a promise that they would not attack the civilian population. The rifle company withdrew, without me, in the direction of Fürstenzell, but was then ordered to return by SS Obersturmbannführer Krüger, to assist in the defense of Passau. I have no knowledge about what happened with the POWs they had with them.

On 23 February 1949, the senior public prosecutor made a request for the arrest of:

(a) Pusch, who in April 1945 was the commander of an SS pioneer training battalion in Passau and who is suspected to have given orders to execute the following Russian POWs: 107 prisoners in the Neuburg Forest and 40 prisoners in Tiefenbach. These prisoners were indeed executed on 26 April 1945, by that same SS unit, as ordered.

(b) Herrmann, Putsch's assistant, was the first, after Moosbauer had ordered to remove the 40 Russians from the town of Tiefenbach, to state that they should be "done in." He suggested this during a meeting with Pusch.

(c) Bischoff, in his role as a close collaborator of General of the Waffen SS von Hassenstein, had given orders on 25 April 1945, from his quarters in Schweiklberg, that 25 Russian POW officers, assigned to the quarry in Neustift, were to be executed. It is assumed that he also played a role in the executions in Passau, given the fact that the POWs in Passau were murdered during the course of the night of 26 April 1945.

Pflaum was responsible for the execution of 25 POWs in Neustift, and performed the executions with the assistance of an SS commando. It is to be assumed that he also played a role during the executions in Passau

Brück, in his role as the defense commissioner of Passau, informed customs officer Stuis and attorney Senninger on 25 or 26 April 1945 that the Russian POWs were to be executed. After the two aforementioned persons refused to follow this order, the POWs were handed over to the SS, who executed them. The reason for the arrest warrants was as follows: "Continued crimes of murder according to section 211 of the penal code."

On 6 December 1949, the senior public prosecutor noted the following:

> During discussions between Senninger and Stuis with Moosbauer, the co-defendant N. Brück participated as well. He was an SS Standartenführer and had been assigned to Moosbauer in April 1945 by deputy Gauleiter Ruckdeschel, apparently because Moosbauer had in some way aroused the ire of the party. As a result it is to be assumed that Brück had a significant influence on the fate of the prisoners. This possibility is all the more plausible since Brück is to have said that he "wanted to see someone hang." In addition Brück had suggested one or two days prior to 26 April 1945, in a comment to the witness Stuis, that the Russians should be murdered. It is significant that Brück was in the possession of a blank passport, which might make it difficult to determine his whereabouts. . . . N. Gröger, SS Standartenführer, was in charge of special assignments and led an SS special command that bore his name; he also had the authority to undersign for the Wehrmacht. N. Jost, supposedly a government official, seems to have presided over the martial court of the SS.

The Perpetrators in Neuburg Forest

Sturmführer Elbl

On 18 May 1945, with the help of interpreter Joe Kuffner, Adolf Gutsch was sworn in. He declared to have known Mr. Elbl for five months. "Elbl was in the 1st training company of the II SS Pi reserve bataillon." In exhibit 14/14a, Adolf Gutsch testified under oath to the following:

> I knew Sturmführer Elbl for five months. Sturmführer Elbl was a member of the 1st Training Company of the Second SS Pioneer Reserve Battalion. I was . . . in the area and was on my way to the Somme Barracks in order to look after the workshop, since I was an electrician by training. There I found Sturmführer Elbl, who seemed extremely tired. When I asked him what was the matter he said: "I've been through quite an ordeal. They got us out of bed in the middle of the night and, on orders from the court-martial officer, they handed out ammunition. Then they were sent off to the Neuburg Forest where they received orders to perform a certain execution. Only after it was over did they know that they were Russian soldiers." Everything I have written here is the truth, so help me God.

Elbl was unable to be found.

Herrmann and Benedix

Maria H., secretary at the Somme Barracks, declared in 1949 to have forwarded a telephone call from Max Moosbauer to the assistant to the commander, Untersturmführer Herrmann. She stated:

> After the conversation ended, Herrmann commented to me that Moosbauer had just told him that were a lot of Russians in Tiefenbach and its vicinity who were to be taken away. He was wondering what to do about it. At that moment three or four SS officers entered the room and Herrmann immediately told them about the case. He informed the officers about the content of his conversation in the same way he had explained it to me. . . . Herrmann asked them the same question regarding what there was to be done about it, and immediately afterward offered his opinion by saying: "It might be best just to go ahead and do them in." He also briefly explained the situation saying that nobody knew where to put these people and that the Americans had already arrived in Tittling. One of the other officers commented that in the case of the other Russians who had been assigned to Hacklberg it had been possible to get them across the Danube. But with the Russians in Tiefenbach this would no longer be possible, because the Americans were already too close. After that Herrmann and the other officers agreed that in the evening a commando of SS men was to be assigned to Tiefenbach to execute the Russians.

Anna K—— from Witzmannsberg near Salzweg was interrogated in her home on 2 January 1951 by Oberkommissar Stadler from the Passau county police; she gave the following statement:

> I cannot give you any information concerning the whereabouts of Hermann Benedix and the other two SS officers. When the Americans marched in, Hermann Benedix spent several nights at my place. At that point I did not know Benedix. He was in the company of two other officers. I do not recall the names of these two officers. I am not acquainted with the previously mentioned Pusch and de Vries. At that point the three officers were disbanded and were staying somewhere in the forested areas around Frauenhof. Eventually they came to my house for shelter. . . . At that time, Benedix, whose name I knew, sent me to go to Frau Br—— in Passau. He wanted Frau Br—— to visit Benedix in Frauenhof. I gave her the message.

Berta Br—— added:

I went with Frau K—— by bicycle and met Untersturmführer Herrmann and Untersturmführer Benedix and another SS officer I only recognize from having seen before. I talked with Benedix. He told me that Herrmann had already been taken prisoner by the Americans, but that he managed to escape by jumping from a truck. Herrmann was lying on a couch and was unable to walk. I asked them what they intended to do. They told me that they wanted to head in the direction of Czechoslovakia. Later Frau K—— told me that the SS officers left on the following day. I cannot say how far they got.

Jungbannführer Erhard

On 22 December 1950, the police interrogated Therese Milaicovic at her home. Her statement about Thomas Erhard was printed as transcript number 3636/50. In it she stated:

Thomas Erhard, born on 4 July 1909, in Unter-Maxdorf, was my tenant from 19 September 1943 until 16 August 1944. As far as I know he was the official Jungbannführer here. One day, I cannot exactly remember the date, probably sometime in the year 1944, he told me that he had to leave because he was being drafted by the military. As far as I know he was a member of the Death's Head SS. I do not know where he went and what he did with the military. If I remember correctly he was wounded and stayed at a field hospital in Passau. I don't remember when he was discharged from the hospital, probably sometime in April 1945. As far as I was told he spent time at the hospital in Freudenhain until 29 June 1945. He visited me several more times at my apartment. My daughter later discovered that the Americans had arrested him at the hospital in Freudenhain on 29 June 1945. I believe that afterwards he spent one and a half years at a camp in Natternberg. After that he moved to Warmensteinach, in the Fichtelgebirge mountains.

In February 1951, Thomas Erhard gave the following statement:

I was SS private of a tank battalion in the 10th Company and was badly wounded in battle near Budapest, on 4 February 1945. I was hospitalized in Passau and stayed there until the end of the war. At the time when the alleged executions took place I was still at the hospital with symptoms of paralysis in my hands and legs. I have no knowledge of what happened during the incident involving the Pioneer Reserve Battalion. It is unclear to me how my name became involved in the criminal proceedings against Moosbauer. Later I served time in an internment camp in Natternberg; I was taken to Natternberg by the CIC directly from the hospital in Passau in May or June.

Hauptsturmführer Schüssler

On 16 April 1951, the engineer Emil Schüssler was interrogated in the town of Schorndorf, near Stuttgart:

> I was drafted into the Wehrmacht in August 1939. In the end I was Captain with the Pioneers. In the fall of 1944 I was ordered to a post with the SS Pioneer Reserve and Training Battalion Number 2, which was stationed at the time in Pikowitz, close to Prague. I came to Passau with this battalion. I had the position of IA [personal assistant]. This did not mean, however, that I was the strategic assistant to the commander; my tasks involved were similar to those of a regional officer. I had the same tasks as Captain Probst, with whom I had worked before. It is true that I wore an SS uniform and insignia, and that my rank was that of an SS Hauptsturmführer.

In reference to the accident involving Pusch, which was mentioned earlier in the report given by Andreas Straßburger, Schüssler testified the following:

> My right arm was in a cast and my chest was bandaged. The following day I drove to Dommelstadel with a car and driver assigned to me and we took quarters with the then mayor. I remained in Dommelstadel until the Americans arrived; I then became a POW of the Americans and was released in the fall of 1945.

What he did not confess to was the following, which Dr. Türk at the Passau hospital personally told me in 1993: Faking an injury, he had approached Dr. Türk during the last few days of the war and pleaded for help. He was fitted with a fake cast and bandages, a disguise that, according to Dr. Türk, fooled the naive American GIs: "They fell for it completely . . . and ultimately showed him mercy."

Defense Commissioner of the Reich, Mayor Max Moosbauer

The 9 December 1947 issue of the *PNP* speculated that in Moosbauer's case "an extradition request by the Russian occupying forces might be considered." But the Soviet Union never arranged trials for anyone and obviously never even made any inquiries—at least not in the case of Max Moosbauer. On 11 August 1950, Max Moosbauer, who was then interned in Eichstätt, stated the following:

In the last weeks before the invasion of the Americans I held the position of defense commissioner of the Reich for the district of Passau. I did not have any particular military authority in this capacity. It was simply a title. . . . I also was leader of the Volkssturm for the Passau district. My capacity in this respect was essentially a formality. The actual business of the Volkssturm was conducted by Captain Stuis, who had his own office. I had nothing to do with regular orders. After the execution of Gauleiter Wächtler on 20 April 1945, a certain district leader by the name of Brück was appointed as a representative of the new Gauleiter, Ruckdeschel. Brück showed me his identification card, which indicated that he was a special commissary with special authorities and a representative of the new Gauleiter. In many matters he acted on his own volition without consulting me. For instance, he had leaflets printed in which he asked for "total resistance" [to the enemy] and threatened that defeatist attitudes would be punishable by death. I only saw these leaflets after they had already been printed. A small portion of them reached the population without any assistance provided by myself. After I became aware of this I made certain that the majority of them were held back and destroyed. As far as I know Brück deserted the Dessau area. Working with Brück was SS standard bearer Herr Jost, who was an administrative lawyer and the chairman of a special court martial. I was not able to find out who co-chaired this court martial, nor was I informed of any court-martial or otherwise involved in any way. There was only one occasion when I accidentally heard about a court-martial against a train conductor and was able to help reach an acquittal of the defendant by arranging for the appearance of a witness for the defense. Another SS standard bearer by the name of Kröger came from the Straubing area at about the same time as Brück and Jost. Kröger had several members of the SS with him who were heavily armed and motorized. I do not know what tasks Kröger was assigned to. He never talked about it. Most of the time he was not in Passau; neither were his people. I do not know what they were doing. Some time before the collapse [of the Third Reich] I transferred the duties of the office of mayor to Dr. Sittler, who then was deputy mayor. I asked him to make certain that he act fully in the interests of the city.

Friedrich Stuis confirmed this statement and added:

There was one time when I talked to Brück at the office of the district leadership, and during this conversation he mentioned something about the fact that the Russians were a burden now and that there was no place for them here any more. This conversation was in reference to the Russian POWs whom Captain Fuhrmann had left behind in Hacklberg. The Russians in question were not only in Hacklberg; there were also some in Jacking, Fatting, Tiefenbach, and in the Lindau area. During my conversation with Brück I had the impression that he was trying to find out how I felt about eliminating the Russians.

Jungbannführer Erhard Thomas stated the following:

> Moosbauer was repeatedly interrogated by the CIC in Natternberg; he was questioned specifically about the execution of Russian POWs. During private conversations with other internees I heard that Moosbauer was said not to have been personally involved with the shootings. The people who told me about this were people who were close to Moosbauer, or who knew him well. I cannot name any specific names, however.

Max Moosbauer was confronted in de-Nazification court with the claim that he had invited four men who were members of the court of justice of the Volk for a lavish dinner in December 1944, covering the expenses, which totaled 400 reichsmarks, with money from city coffers. This while supposedly not having enough money to feed the Russians. Mossbauer remained silent and provided no answers or explanation.

Stuis

Customs officer Fritz Stuis was deemed by the court to be a simple "participator," and merely had to pay a fine of one hundred deutschmarks.

Gaida

Anton Wallner recalled:

> I was told by some of his Russians after the invasion of the Americans that Gaida was killed by being shot thirty-three times by several of his Russians in a place called Eholfing. It was fairly well known that a woman by the name of Maria Schuster, a homemaker from Hacklberg, number 24, had been Gaida's mistress. Therefore it is likely that she knew quite a bit about what was happening in this camp. Every now and then she even accompanied Gaida to the camp.

Maria Schuster, however, was never called as a witness.

Bischoff

Anneliese W. stated in 1950 that

One of the people who worked very closely with Hassenstein was a major by the name of Ernst Bischoff. His wife, G. Bischoff, told me in the fall of 1945 or 1946, or it could have been sometime after Christmas, that her husband had been killed by foreigners in Wendelstein, a town in the vicinity of Nuremberg.

Pusch

On 17 May 1945, at 11 P.M. the American officer Dwight McKay took Obersturmbannführer Friedrich Pusch of the Waffen SS to the Passau county prison. On 24 November 1950, Pusch was interrogated before the district court for criminal offences in Vienna. He stated, among other things:

> As of 1944 I was commander of the SS Pioneer training battalion. It was my task to train the battalion and I had absolutely no authority to give orders to my troops or any other units that were not in some way connected to their training. I therefore deny very strongly ever having given orders for the execution of Russian POWs on 29 April 1945, as well as anytime before or after that date. I did not even known that there ever were any Russian prisoners in Tiefenbach or in the Neuburg Forest. . . . At the end of April and the beginning of May 1945, I no longer held the position of commander of the Pioneer training battalion. One day during the second half of April 1945, I don't recall the exact day, I was badly wounded while driving in my car on official business.

On 5 December 1950, he added:

> The next day I was sent to be with my family in Egelsee, about twelve kilometers from Passau, to be cared for at home. As of that moment, or rather as of the day of my being sent home after being wounded, I effectively was no longer in charge of the commando of the SS Pioneer training battalion, nor did I have any further contact with it after that time. . . . About three weeks later, when I had just started to be able to stand up and move around again inside the house, I was arrested by the American CIC and brought to their headquarters; they were stationed in a castle. There I spent about eight to ten days, during which time the CIC made extensive inquiries about me. Since there was no incriminating evidence against me I was brought to an internment camp in Natternberg, as were other members of the SS and National Socialists. From there I was taken to various camps; the last one was in Glasenbach, from where I was transferred to the district court for criminal

offences in Vienna; this was in August 1947, and after one week I was released upon my word.

General Hassenstein

Anneliese W. gave the following statement in the year 1950:

> From the end of 1942 until 1945 I was the secretary to General Inspector for Hitler Army Recruits, General von Hellermann. To my knowledge Hassenstein remained commander of combat training facility number 1 of the infantry in Dresden until the end of 1944. He was then transferred to the service of General von Hellermann and was there named commander of the infantry school. In April 1945 that department was transferred from Potsdam to Vilshofen, on the Danube. At the time of the collapse [of the Third Reich] General Hassenstein left the department along with several former staff people. . . . As far as Frau Hassenstein told me back then in Vilshofen, her husband killed himself. I have no knowledge as to the whereabouts of Frau Hassenstein at the present moment.

Karl Probst, an officer of the Wehrmacht in Passau who held the rank of captain, describes Hassenstein as follows:

> At one point a messenger sent by General Hassenstein brought a letter addressed to the senior officer of the Wehrmacht. I opened the letter, as this was within my authority. I could see that in this letter he did not accept a judgment by the Passau court martial of the Wehrmacht that had sentenced a defendant to a hefty prison term; the judgment seemed too lenient to him. I remember very well that he declared that in the future he would make sure that officers who passed such weak sentences would be court-martialed themselves.

Dr. Rolf Massow declared in 1950:

> Toward the end of the war I was assigned to the Hassenstein division, which was just being assembled at the time. His staff was then stationed in Schweiklberg, near Vilshofen. I did not know General Hassenstein at that point. I knew him for only about fourteen days and did not have much to do with him. . . . A few days before the fighting ended, the staff quarters were moved from Schweiklberg into a forest ranger's house close by. One day before his death Hassenstein had already alluded to the fact that he would be ending his life. At that time he even ordered me to shoot him. Of course I refused. According to rumors I later heard from others it seems clear that Hassenstein had asked several other officers to

do the same. He even seems to have issued a written order to that effect. We were aware of the fact that Hassenstein had intended to kill both himself and his wife on the day in question and we also knew that he was planning to do this in the cellar of his quarters. If I remember correctly, Hassenstein fired into his mouth and was dead immediately. In the case of his wife the gun malfunctioned. . . . I do not believe that other persons could be implicated in the death of Herr Hassenstein. I had the impression that the general was very dejected about the hopelessness of his situation, especially since he also had become disabled and that this is why he chose a self-inflicted death. He was buried there immediately afterwards. His wife attended the funeral.

After decades of silence, the 27 June 1991 issue of the *PNP* reported on page 23 that in the case of Hassenstein's suicide "could not be ruled out." The present owners of the mansion in which the Hassensteins had lived, however, found Hassenstein immediately after having heard the shot; one family member stated: "The way he was sitting there, with the gunshot wound in his head—it's impossible that he committed suicide. There's no way." Today he is buried at the so-called graveyard of heroes in downtown Passau where his grave is marked with his own personal memorial stone. The grave was built and is taken care of by the German War Grave Welfare Organization. Perhaps more macabre is the fact that the Central Organization for Political Education in Bavaria as well as the City of Passau refer to this very cemetery as being the "Memorial for the Victims of National Socialism."

Postscript

To this day nothing in the Neuburg Forest recalls the massacres that took place there during the final days of the war. The place where Russian POWs were forced to dig their own graves before they were killed in cold blood today houses a children's playground and a picnic area. Approximately seven hundred Russians were killed on this site. In 1956, following another process of exhumation, the remains of 107 Russian POWs were transferred to a cemetery in Neumarkt, in the Upper Palatinate region of Bavaria. While there is no memorial to these Russian dead, the site in the Neuburg Forest is marked by a large memorial stone built in honor of a certain forest ranger by the name of Ahr, who exerted his influence to support the construction of the playground. It is readily apparent that no one wishes to be reminded of the fact that sixty years ago Russian POWs were slaughtered at this very place.

The Neustift Quarry: The Massacre of Russian Officers

In April 1945 in Nammering, twenty-five Russian officers were taken from their jobs at the company of Rieger and Seil and were brought to the Neustift quarry, which was owned by the same company, about fifteen kilometers west of Passau, where they were forced to perform slave labor. The quarry was approximately five kilometers south of Vilshofen, and Max Wagner, who lived in that town, remembered shortly before his death in 1992:

> One of the prisoners, a major who spoke German, was allowed to walk down to the city sometimes and buy things. Hans Grätzer, who owned the watch shop in Vilshofen, can attest to this. The major had watches repaired there on several occasions, which meant that there was no reason to fear repercussions of any kind. Just a few days after the transfer of the Russians, however, Josef Seil, the director of the company Rieger and Seil, is said to have informed the SS in Schweiklberg that no food provisions were left and that the Russians should be picked up. On 25 April 1945, Major Bischoff, the personal associate of General Hassenstein, called back and gave orders to execute the Russians.

Herr Pflaum, also a major of the Waffen SS in Schweiklberg and in Passau, followed through on this order during the night of 25 to 26 April, with the help of an SS commando. The Russian officers were first forced to climb into a truck. They had to lie face down and were taken to the edge of the forest in the vicinity of Zeitlarn. There they had to dig their own graves before they were marched into the forest and shot. Several people who lived in the neighborhood started hearing shots around 4 A.M. Lina Steidl from Oberzeitlarn recalled:

> Our house in Oberzeitlarn is located about fifty meters away from the mass grave of the Russian officers, and about 150 to 200 meters from the place where they were shot in the forest, in 1945. It was in the early morning hours of 26 April 1945 when I awoke from my sleep and heard shots in the nearby forest. Since the Americans were not too far off at this time I initially believed that it was the Americans arriving. But then I kept hearing more and more shots, and in the end it sounded as though a machine gun was being fired. It must have been around 4:00 A.M. when all this was happening. I got up at about 4:30 A.M. and looked out toward the street. I saw German soldiers standing around. They also were standing along the two paths leading to the nearby forest. I stayed in the house and at 7:00 A.M. my husband returned from his job

at the prison in Unteriglbach, where he worked as the warden. He asked me if I knew what all the soldiers were doing here . . . and he told me that they were SS soldiers.

The mayor of Zeitlarn at that time, Max Paul, who also was woken up by the shots at about 4 A.M., recalled:

> I thought that maybe the paratroopers had landed, since the Americans weren't far away at that time. During the course of the day the farmer Herr Striedl from Oberroh came by and told me that he had seen a Russian cap and traces of blood on the path leading to his property. He said that something must have happened, because they had kept shooting early in the morning. We didn't know any details about what had taken place.

Alois Striedl, the owner of the Einödhof farm, which is located about four hundred meters from the site of the massacre, was just on his way to go hunting. On 18 July 1950, Oberwachtmeister Kuas of the county police for crimes at the main station in Vilshofen visited him at his home and wrote an interrogation protocol. Striedl stated therein that he, too, heard machine gun fire. He saw a Russian run out of the forest, flee across the field, and then disappear in the brush. Thirty minutes later he heard more shots. At 5:30 A.M. a maid told him that the guards had only let her pass through the forest after she had told them that she was going to work. Minutes later two French prisoners found a trail of blood. When Striedl went to check the location himself, he found a Russian cap. He also heard noises that sounded as though people were working with shovels and pick-axes at a nearby gravel pit. His sister saw some members of the SS carrying away piles of clothes. At about 8 P.M. Striedl drove to Vilshofen where he saw another truck and one soldier. Several hours later he discovered a freshly dug-up pit.

Lina Steidl witnessed the following:

> The SS soldiers stayed there for about three days. On the second and third days many of them began to leave and only a few guards remained stationed at the edge of the forest. After the second day we didn't see any SS men at all. On the fourth day, 30 April 1945, I heard from Frau Kreitl, who now lives in Plattling and at that time was living on the Striedl's farm, that Russians were supposedly buried in the forest. I said to Frau Kreitl that when they were shooting in the morning, a few days ago, that it could have been the Russians they were shooting. When the SS soldiers had all left I took a sack and pretended to go collect pinecones

in the forest. I wanted to see the place where the Russians were said to lay buried. Frau Kreitl and I went into the forest together and as we approached the gravel pit we came across a freshly dug-up area, which had already been overgrown by plants. After we saw where the mass grave was we went back home. The next day the Americans arrived. I had decided to immediately report to the Americans that there was a Russian mass grave in the forest. But I didn't get the chance, because two Russians had escaped the shooting and they told the Americans themselves.

The Americans Are Coming

Following an order by General Hassenstein, the Danube Bridge in Vilshofen was blown up on 29 April 1945. The Vils Bridge and the railway crossing remained intact, because courageous citizens had pulled the bombs off with the help of a tractor. The planned destruction of the railway crossing did not take place because the employee in charge refused to hand over the plans. The official state newspaper, which only a few days before had proclaimed the final victory, was no longer printed. The mayor of Vilshofen, Herr Willeitner, suffered a nervous breakdown. The first American tanks were approaching. The Americans had already passed through Osterhofen and changed direction toward the town of Gergweis. When SS troops retreated across the Vils Bridge they came under fire by the Americans. In Sandbach, a few kilometers to the southeast of Vilshofen, the flak unit, which had been posted at the train station since 19 March, was pulled back and roadblocks were set up at the town center. Three artillery pieces were set up at the edge of the forest with the purpose of stopping the progress of the tanks. An SS unit that had been brought in from the south took part in the battle, and shot and killed an American medical orderly.

On 1 May 1945 at 5 P.M., Vilshofen surrendered unconditionally following orders by the NSDAP district leadership. Battle commander König had already been informed of the capitulation when a second American soldier was ambushed and shot. Approximately 1,800 American occupying soldiers were billeted. On 9 May a jeep was driven through town with the juice manufacturer Hans Helling tied to the hood of the vehicle. Josef Schlager and Ludwig Mielach were taken into custody by an MP by the name of Jacks and a Henry Robert, who had recently been liberated from a concentration camp. The former SA Hauptsturmführer

Hans Schedlbauer was shot and killed by Jacks. Schlager was able to escape. The blacksmith Josef Paul recalled that he and his father were

> alerted by the French POWs who worked with us that something had happened in the forest. We didn't know what it could be. I only found out about the whole thing and the Russian mass graves when they started digging. People from the community of Zeitlarn had to dig them up and lay them out on a meadow at the edge of the forest. As I was looking at the dead bodies, I noticed at that point that in some cases their sexual organs were missing, most likely as a result of having been shot off or mutilated. The local men who were in charge of digging up the bodies were to be shot afterwards, as revenge for the murder of the Russians.

Just the Thought of It Terrified Me

The mayor of Vilshofen, Max Paul, recalled in 1950:

> Only after the Americans began marching in did people start saying that something must have happened in the forest near the Steidl place. I went into the forest with a few neighbors, and when we arrived, several Russians were already there. One of them told us in broken German that Russians had been executed and buried there. A short time later more Russians appeared. They surrounded me and threatened to shoot me because they thought that I, as mayor, had known about this. They knew that I was mayor and wanted to hold me responsible for the execution. Two refugees who spoke Russian explained to them what had happened and that I was innocent. I sent my son to the military government in Vilshofen to get help [to protect us from these threats].

Paul Jr. recalls: "Only after I explained to them that [the Mayor and some others] really were in grave danger did the Americans agree to come with me to Zeitlarn. They disarmed the Russians and from then on all was quiet." Lina Steidl remarked:

> The Americans had been here for a while already and the Russians had already started digging when [Josef Seil] disappeared for a few weeks. There were rumors that the Russians were planning to kill [Seil] because they assumed that [Seil] was responsible for the shootings. . . . The exhumed bodies of the Russians were reburied in the new mass grave on the way from Vilshofen to Ortenburg, in Oberzeitlarn. My father, who saw the exhumed Russians, told me that on some of them the genitals were missing, and that others had their arms and legs cut

off. I myself didn't look, because just the thought of it terrified me. . . .
That's all I can say about the matter. My statements are the truth and
nothing but the truth.

Other witnesses said that in some cases the eyes, ears, noses, and tongues
of the murdered were mutilated or cut off.

The Investigations by the District Attorney's Office

On 23 February 1949, the Passau district attorney noted the following:

> According to . . . witness interrogations, SS Major Bischoff, in his role
> as the IA of the SS General von Hassenstein, issued the order, on 25
> April 1945, that the twenty-five Russian officers who were accommo-
> dated at the quarry in Neustift were to be executed. He gave this order
> by phone. During the night of 26 April, SS Major Pflaum arrived in
> Neustift with an SS commando and had the POWs executed there.

On 9 May, five years after the murders, district attorney Stögmayer wrote
the following to the examining magistrate Dr. Leiss: "It has been known
for quite some time that at the end of April 1945, twenty-four Russian
officers who were POWs were executed by the SS in the Neustift/Vil-
shofen quarry. Investigations were conducted in this case, however a thor-
ough examination has not been possible, partly due the lack of a German
jurisdiction." On 12 July 1950, District Court Councilor Dr. Leiss wrote
to the headquarters of the county police in Vilshofen: "The investigations
conducted in Neustift/Ortenburg did not lead to any significant findings.
. . . I am requesting appropriate action be taken [and that the investigation
be intesified]." Three days later Dr. Leiss claimed that the residents only
heard about the murders a week after they had happened. "Some thought
the Americans had arrived, others assumed that paratroopers had landed."
The investigation was discontinued two years later. The extant files, however, mention that fact that the Americans caught and executed the person who in their eyes bore the main responsibility for the Russian murders.
His name is not mentioned in the German files.

"Participator" Josef Seil

On 21 November 1947, the *PNP* reported that the hearing against Josef
Seil, the fifty-nine-year-old director and partner of the Lower Bavarian
gravel company Rieger and Seil in Neustift/Vilshofen, had been resumed.
It was the most extensive hearing Vilshofen had ever experienced and lasted

for three days. Seventy-five witnesses had been called and the courtroom was packed. In May 1947 Josef Seil had been labeled a mere "participator" in the events. In the months that followed, however, new documents surfaced: Seil was identified as having been a member of the NSDAP since as early as 1933; he had also been a member of the NSKK (National Social-ist Motorcar Corps) as of 1935 where he had served as "district economic advisor"—an "influential role." The *PNP* titled the report: "OPPORTUNIS-TIC PARTY MEMBER." But because Josef Seil gave the court the impression of having been "generous," he was again relabeled as just a participator.

A Memorial for the Victims

Along the street leading from Vilshofen to Ortenburg, where today a wooden signpost advertises a local fish farm, the mass grave used to be located. Max Wagner wrote in 1992:

> In the context of the repatriation efforts for POWs, three Russian offi-cers came to the Vilshofen city hall in May 1945. They asked to speak to the officials in charge and said that . . . they had already acquired a gravestone and asked to have an appropriate inscription engraved on it. The official tried to comply with their wish. He cannot remember the exact wording of the inscription but it was something like: "IN MEMORY OF THOSE WHO DIED FOR THEIR COUNTRY."

The memorial stone was made of granite. It was located alongside the street. In 1956 the mass grave was reopened. The remains of the mur-dered Russians were transferred to Neumarkt in the Upper Palatinate region of Bavaria. The community asked to have the memorial stone to place in its cemetery. But Herr Steidl had moved more quickly, insisting that since the stone was located on his land, that he should keep it for him-self. One can see it to this day—it forms a part of the wall behind his house. That's where Steidl had it cemented in, with the inscription facing inwards.

The Camps of Tiefenbach, Jacking, and Fatting: Starved, Beaten, and Shot and Killed

Ludwig Kreipl, a teacher and former NSDAP regional leader in a com-munity about five kilometers north of Passau, stated during an interroga-tion before the district attorney's office in Passau on 28 August 1950 that in early March 1945 he was informed via the railway headquarters of Pas-sau that 1,200 Russian POWs were to arrive in Tiefenbach. He objected to this plan. The first two hundred arrived in the middle of March, another four hundred followed soon after. Frau Katharina Lindner, a housewife, recorded in her journal that on 28 March, three camps holding approximately seven hundred Russian prisoners were established in Tiefenbach and the neighboring communities of Jacking and Fatting. Before arriving there, the Russians had been marching on foot since January, having previously worked in various mines.

The prisoners were guarded by soldiers of the Wehrmacht from Upper Silesia and by the members of the Tiefenbach Volkssturm. Food was provided by the administration of the prison camp in Hacklberg, which was overseen by a Captain Fuhrmann. Katharina Lindner described many of the Russians as "ill, exhausted, and broken-down" when they arrived. One of them was Anton Antoniewicz Micheda. In the Russian statement he provided authorities on 24 May 1945, later translated into English by Frank S. Udiski and would later be included as part of exhibit 8, he gave the following sworn written testimony:

I was taken prisoner on 11 May 1942, in the city of Bytum in Poland. The number of my POW unit was 100. The German officer in charge was Sergeant Kapica, a corporal. His unit had the number 398. On 22 January 1945, we began our march into Germany. We were given nothing to eat or drink during the twenty days the march lasted, all the way from Bytum into Czechoslovakia. Originally a total of 386 of our people started out on the march; when we arrived in Tiefenbach, only 184 of us were left. Those of us who had become too weak were simply shot by the side of the road, as were those who asked for food or water or attempted to get it themselves. On the first day we arrived in Czechoslovakia—I don't remember the date—people were allowed to give us food and water, but the next day this was prohibited. So they left food and water for us by the roadside. We were not allowed to pick it up, but some of us were lucky enough to get our hands on some of it. The Czech civilians and the police behaved decently toward us during the three weeks the march lasted. As soon as we crossed the border from Czechoslovakia into Germany the Germans got much tougher; they beat us and shot several of us who had picked up water and food. We arrived in Tiefenbach on 22 March 1945. Sergeant Kapica and fifteen of his Nazi soldiers brought us to a barracks that was basically a stable. We worked in the vicinity of Passau repairing bomb damage and filling bomb craters. Our overseers beat us whenever we tried to rest. Each day we received a bowl of so-called soup as our ration.

Bokow Wasilew, also a former POW, wrote his statement on 25 May 1945 with the help of Frank S. Udiski. The testimony was translated into English and would later be included as part of exhibit 7. In it we read:

> We arrived at the Tiefenbach camp on 27 March 1945; we were given very little food and were beaten frequently. We had to walk to Passau to work there, and were barely given any food while working. All we got was a liter of soup—not a single ounce of bread. The prisoners became so weak that they were barely able to walk from one place to the next. They sent several of the prisoners to work for German farmers.

Most of the prisoners had to work for the national rail of the Reich, laying rails or preparing railroad ties. Some of them worked in the town of Schalding, others had to march all the way to Passau to help with the cleanup there. The so-called "Handbook for Leaders of Work Commandos," edited by the commander of prisoners of war of the Wehrkreis XIII, contained fifty pages on how to deal with the prisoners. A copy exists to this day at the Bundesarch-Militärarchiv in Freiburg under the document number RH 49/24. The section entitled "Special Regulations for Soviet Prisoners of War" specifies among other things:

> ACCOMMODATIONS: the accommodations for Soviet POWs have to be especially carefully secured and controlled. Windows must be secured with iron bars or iron grilles, and the doors must be padlocked. The accommodation has to have separate access; rooms and latrines must be separated by wooden partitions in order to prevent exchanges with other persons. An area fenced in by barbed wire is imperative. The Stalag will deliver barbed wire for a charge. For this purpose, a precise map as well as a verifiable amount of material must be included in orders submitted by the contractors. The basic measurements for one meter of fence with a height of 2.5 meters equals 16 meters of barbed wire, which is the maximum allowance. All security measures for accommodations must be carefully checked every day. Alarms and other security measures against threats by fire or air attack must be installed; instructions for conduct must be established for each work commando and must be practiced with the prisoners of war. Heating of the rooms must be sufficient, since otherwise there will be insufficient utilization of nutrients and a tendency to illnesses; illnesses will result in an unacceptable loss of workforce.

In Passau and its vicinity, however, it seems that not even these requirements were met.

Daily Life in Oberjacking

The people who ran the Knott Inn in Oberjacking, a small village close to Tiefenbach, were ordered to accommodate approximately one hundred Russian POWs in their barn. French and Polish POWs had already been quartered for quite some time in the second floor of the restaurant. There were two Russian women, Nadja and Ludmilla, who were almost part of the family and who spoke some German. Wehrmacht soldiers belonging to the Fuhrmann commando from Upper Silesia were guarding the prisoners. Sergeant Schuh was particularly vicious and used to say: "These riffraff deserve everything they're getting!"

There was a deep trench dug all around the perimeter of the barn and covered with wooden boards; this was the latrine. Only every fourteen days were the Russians allowed to wash themselves in the lake that belonged to the house. If, due to exhaustion, one of them slipped while kneeling down or if a second person stumbled over him they were mercilessly beaten with rubber clubs. The Russians were given next to nothing to eat and many died of starvation. Officially the reasons for their deaths were quite different, of course. Even through there was never a physician or a forensic pathologist called in to check on the dead, work commando leader Sergeant Schuh reported to the registry office in Tiefenbach such causes of death as pleurisy and heart disease. The youngest prisoner to have died was twenty-five years old; the oldest was a week shy of his forty-fifth birthday.

Those Russians who had died of hunger or had been beaten to death were simply dragged up to the second floor of the inn, where they were placed on wooden boards stretched between two beer barrels until the corpses were ultimately taken away. It was intended that the foreign forced laborers and the innkeepers would see these dead; indeed, they continued to live in these rooms and even ate and slept in close proximity to them. There was a new body to be found almost every day.

German mothers whose sons had been drafted and sent to Russia would sometimes throw some bread to the prisoners. But God forbid they should be discovered! Kathie Reitinger still remembers how an older woman who had been caught doing so was taken up to the second floor of the inn and beaten so badly she was barely able to walk afterwards. She recalled:

> The poor men were lying in the barn, close to death and in horrible condition. They had nothing to eat and many were very sick. Every few days another one would die. The guards treated the Russians very brutally; to

them they were subhuman creatures. The POWs from France or Poland were better off; they lived in the inn and were fed more often. The Russians were beaten and tortured; it was horrible. We slipped them things to eat as often as we could, and I saw them scarf down pig feed on more than one occasion; that's how hungry they were. It was heart wrenching to see. They were allowed to wash themselves in the lake only every two weeks, and even then they were tortured and beaten. I would like to see Ludmilla again, the Russian woman; these people were so unfortunate; and they were people just like us; it was terrible.

Because the owners of the restaurant, the Knott family, did not have much money and the inn was not doing well financially, and because they could not bear to witness the prisoners' misery any longer, they left potato peels and other leftovers from the kitchen outside at the entrance. The Russian POWs would greedily devour these scraps. The owner at the time, Babette Knott, was desperately hoping that somebody would be helping her sons Josef and Clemens in the same way; they were soldiers in Russia at that time. She never reported it when, every once in a while, a hen would disappear and a Polish forced laborer admitted that he had taken it out of hunger and had shared it with his girlfriend. She even let the couple have a quiet room in the second floor, where every now and then they had an opportunity to meet other foreigners as well.

Hunger in Fatting

In the barn belonging to the Köberl couple in nearby Fatting, 182 Russians were quartered; the barn remains almost unchanged to this day. The farmer couple could see how weakened and emaciated these people were, and cooked bucketfuls of flour soup for them. Frequently the prisoners spilled the soup, as they were so hungry that they grabbed the plates so greedily that the bowls slipped out of their hands. It was obvious that the Russians who had to cook for everyone were well fed and in good shape, while the others were extremely thin. Six of them died of starvation. Sergeant Lipka, the leader of the work commando, reported rather imaginative reasons for their deaths, even though it was mandatory to consult a physician to determine cause of death. He went so far as refusing to entering the date of birth on the death certificates.

The Removal of the Corpses: Buried in Wrapping Paper

Katharina Lindner wrote the following in her notebook: "One by one they died, and there were forty graves at the [Tiefenbach] cemetery; after that the Russians were buried in the sports field. The locals had sympathy for them and, whenever possible, gave them potatoes, bread, and flour, even though everything was very scarce." Deaths among the Russians were reported to the Tiefenbach registry office up until 2 May 1945. Only thirty-eight of the dead are known by name. A total of thirty-four corpses were buried at the edge of the forest, west of Leithen; seventeen were buried at the Tiefenbach cemetery; and forty-three in the former sports fields, south of Weideneck. It is not clear to either the local community administration or to witnesses what the criteria for this "distribution" actually was. Most likely the ones who died in Fatting and Jacking were buried in Leithen, the ones from Tiefenbach at the cemetery. And when the cemetery was full—but the deaths continued—the corpses were simply disposed of a bit farther away, in the sports field. The "Handbook for Leaders of Work Commandos" explicitly states:

> In its dealings with the Soviet Union, the Reich is not bound by the Geneva Agreement. . . . Guards will be authorized to use their weapons (rifle butt, rifle, pistol) . . . under the following conditions: to prevent escape; if the POW does not stop after "Halt!" has been called out three times, fire will be opened with the intention of hitting the escapee. In the case of Soviet POWs this will be the case without calling out any warning; this also applies for escape attempts of prisoners of other nationalities.
>
> For Russian POWs the following special regulations are in force: Funerals will take place in total silence; Muslims are to be buried with their heads pointing east and their faces pointing south; a German military delegation will not be assigned; the participation of comrades of the deceased who belong to the same work commando is allowed; civilians are not allowed to participate; priests or clerical assistants may participate as long as they belong to the same work commando; deceased Soviets do not receive a coffin, but are buried instead in reenforced wrapping paper or in paper sacks; there will be no wreaths, the graves will not be decorated; no photographs of the grave sites will be taken.

On Tuesday, 24 April 1945, it was announced that the group of guards had marched off in a southern direction, taking with them thirty Russians and the entire food supply. The stonemason Josef Höldl and the teacher Herr Kreipl demanded that Fuhrmann should take back the remaining prisoners. He, however, threatened that the Russians would be returned to Tiefenbach if they had indeed been deported to Hacklberg. Kreipl then drove by himself to the district leader of Passau, Moosbauer. Moosbauer later recalled that Kreipl "was complaining about the fact that the prisoners who were unable to march . . . were attacking . . . the population. . . . He begged me desperately to get rid of the Russians." As a result Moosbauer asked for help from the SS at the Passau Somme Barracks and "demanded" the Russians' deportation "in the interest of security." He conceded, however, that he might have said that he "did not care what the SS did with the Russians, even if they decided to shoot them." According to Kreipl, Moosbauer even said to send the Russians to the Neuburg Forest with saws, shovels, and pickaxes to build entrenchments and tank ditches. The fact remains, however, that in the Jacking camp, Kreipl gave orders to send all Russians to Hacklberg or to the Maierhof Barracks. They began to march in that direction. The Russians from Fatting were transferred to Passau as well. The sick and those unable to walk were taken away on carts. On 28 August 1950 Ludwig Kreipl was finally interrogated about these matters under oath. Landgerichtsrat Dr. Leiss served as investigating judge and listed his statement in transcript number 22/49, file AVZ 2 Js 3612/46.

In Tiefenbach it was a different story : the stonemason Herr Höldl and Mayor Moser had agreed with the district administrator to send twenty Russians each to the neighboring communities and to hand them over once the Americans arrived. This did actually take place. Only the community of Ruderting refused to accept them and sent "its" Russians back to Tiefenbach; there were now altogether forty deathly ill Russians in Tiefenbach. Some of the ones still able to walk could be housed with farmers. On Thursday, 26 April 1945, a fighting unit of the SS intended to "kill them all" on their own. Kreipl later suggested that "this might have been due to complaints by [German] refugees from Silesia, who felt they were being shortchanged in their food supply because of the Russians."

Marching toward Death

Anton Antoniewicz Micheda recalled the following:

> On 27 April and in the early morning of 28 April, Sergeant Kapica and ten German soldiers took twenty-seven of my friends and left town with them without any explanation. . . . Originally there were 184 of us in the Tiefenbach camp and then three comrades died. So then we were 181. As I said before, twenty-seven of them were taken away; today we know that they were murdered. Then we were 154. Of those, 106 were able to hide without being caught. They were hiding in the surrounding

hills. A total of forty-eight of us Russian POWs and slave laborers remained in Tiefenbach. On Saturday, 28 April 1945, the head of guard personnel declared that all Russians were to be transferred to the camp in Sulzbach on the Inn River. However, there were no carts available for the numerous sick. The ones from the villages of Fatting and Jacking who were able to walk were also ordered to begin marching in the direction of Passau and most likely were executed at the Inn quay, together with the twenty-seven Russians from Tiefenbach. The perpetrators were members of the Second SS Pioneer Training Battalion from the Somme Barracks, which was for a short time incorporated into the Oberdonau Task Force. When the prisoners disappeared, so did the guard personnel with the entire, already scarce, food provisions. In Jacking, the proprietress of the Knott Inn and her daughter accommodated the sick prisoners in the main room of the restaurant. In order to survive, however, the prisoners had to go begging, since food supplies were extremely limited.

Franz Xaver Köberl from Fatting also had prisoners stay in his house, where the guards had been living up to that point. He provided them with food as best as he could.

Yesterday Hitler Youth, Today Mayor

Anton Antoniewicz Micheda gave the following sworn statement shortly after the end of the war:

> The remaining four German soldiers left to guard us at Tiefenbach, said we were on our own now because they had nothing to do with us as of this day. There were 159 of us left at Tiefenbach. However when any of us Russians took off, Ludwig Rankl who is a bookkeeper at present in the Burgermeister's office, with his armed band of Hitler Youth brought us back and has us shot without trial.

The files reveal no further details. However, this testimony was confirmed by one of his fellow victims named Bokow. Today Ludwig Rankl is mayor of Tiefenbach.

Ivan Ivanovic Savelyeu from Kuleshavo (in the vicinity of Gorbacheosky) later signed the following affidavit in the presence of U.S. Army Captain Kenneth R. Wilson:

> I was placed in that camp, but I didn't work outside during the time I was there. The mayor of Tiefenbach frequently turned to the SS with the request to remove the prisoners from the camp. Late in the evening

of 28 April 1945, an SS officer drove up in a car and saw that the prisoners in the camp were sick and exhausted; he then told the commander
and the mayor of Tiefenbach that the Russian prisoners could stay
where they were because they were so worn out.

On 29 April 1945, the mayor complained again to the SS fighting troops
saying that it was time for the prisoners to be removed from Tiefenbach.
Katharina Lindner noted: "Some of the farmers were hiding their Russians and so they couldn't remove many of them; only the sick ones
remained." Gertraud Gibl provided a written statement on 25 May 1945.
Sergeant Jan Fenijn provided the English translation, which would later
be included as exhibit 3. Gibl, who was nineteen at the time, stated that
on 29 April 1945, at approximately 5:45 in the evening, a truck carrying
about fifteen SS soldiers arrived in Tiefenbach and stopped near the small
store belonging to the Bauer family. "I saw the SS soldiers jump down
from the truck with shovels in their hands; they asked Alois Bauer where
the Russian camp was located." Alois Bauer showed them the way, as did
Anni Knott. Anton Antoniewicz Micheda explained: "We noticed that the
mayor was collecting shovels and spades, while fifteen SS men arrived in
Tiefenbach by car. I became suspicious and escaped. I was one of the lucky
ones who lived to tell this story . . . only six people survived." Savelyeu was
one of them: "When all of us had arrived in the barracks the fifteen SS
men came in and yelled 'Russians, get up!'" Adults and children were
looking on. Gertrud Gibl states: "I watched the SS men order the Russians to leave; they carried their sick comrades out of the camp. The SS
soldiers were carrying rifles. I also saw all of the prisoners and the SS soldiers leave in the direction of Hochholz."

Johann Rankl (a relative of today's mayor of Tiefenbach, Ludwig Rankl),
however, stated:

> After they [the SS] arrived I heard shots being fired from the direction
> of the Russian camp. When I went there I was threatened by an SS sol-
> dier with a rifle and I was denied access to the camp. I went home and
> about ten minutes later a child asked me to go over to the Knott Inn.
> The same SS soldier who had threatened me with the rifle asked me
> whether I was bearing any messages written by the Russians who were
> staying with the farmers. I told him "no" and went home.

In the meantime horrible things were happening at the barracks. Aleksejew Michajew Andres was there and lived through it all. On 24 May 1945

Andres provided his written statement. It was translated into English by Corporal Joseph Sabolesky and later included as part of exhibit 2. In it Andres stated: "The SS started to chase us out of the camp. We didn't get out fast enough, so the SS fired above our heads and chased us out by beating us with rubber clubs. They made us move in rows of three. There were forty-six of us and two more joined us from some farm houses, so that altogether we were forty-eight." Ivan Ivanovich Savelyeu added: "All of the sick and worn out prisoners slowly started to get up and the SS started to shoot into the air in order to make them move faster. In the haste, many of the exhausted fell down to the floor while getting out of the upper bed bunks. Soon everybody was running out of the barracks. The SS gave every group of seven men one shovel each. They also gave us three or four pickaxes." Bokow Wasilew reported: "On 29 April 1945, at about 6 P.M. . . . we had to line up in groups of three. I saw that the SS had four shovels. They had us march into the forest. As we were walking the SS men went into the houses [we passed] where they picked up additional shovels." Savelyeu added:

> I was walking behind the group, carrying a sick man. We were walking toward the forest. The SS men had told us that if anybody turned around to look, or even just looked to the side, that that person would be shot. There were forty-six of us in the barracks. There also was an interpreter and one commander, and later the SS brought two people who had been staying with the tailor and the blacksmith. The SS led us to the edge of the forest; when we arrived I set down the sick man I had been carrying and started to run into the forest. The head of the SS men there ordered his soldiers to shoot at me. They opened fire but I was able to get away; while running I threw off my shoes and my clothes. I stayed in the forest the whole day and the night and the next day, naked and hungry.

The Massacre in the Tiefenbach Hochholz Forest

Bokow Wasilew continued:

> When we came to the forest the officer ordered us to remain standing at the edge of the forest. Five minutes later he came back with several others and told his soldiers to take us to the place from which they had just returned. They selected ten of us and handed each a spade. The officer told us if we walked fast he would give us cigarettes. He gave each of us a cigarette and then he had us dig a hole. We dug one, and

started a second one, and we finished that one, too. Then we saw that they were leading some of the sick people to the hole and having them look into it with their faces down. Then the soldiers shot every single one of them. We who had dug the hole were made to cover the dead with overcoats and quickly spread some dirt over them. Then they brought a second group up to the second hole and shot them, too.

A third hole followed. Aleksejew Michajew Andres related: "Then we began to dig a second grave. The soldiers shot four groups of our people." Bokow Wasilew stated: "Then we started to dig a pit for ourselves. Before we were able to finish it the soldiers had us cover up the dead in the other pits. Before we had finished that the soldiers ordered us to position ourselves around the pit. It was already getting dark. That's when we fled." Andres, too, succeeded in escaping:

When they began to shoot the last group, four of us fled into the forest. As we were escaping the soldiers fired at us and killed one person; three of us continued to run. As we were running the soldiers started running after us, but lucky for us it was beginning to get dark and it was raining slightly. I ran about two hundred meters and fortunately found a large tree lying on the ground. I hid under it for about thirty minutes. The soldiers were screaming and shooting; then everything grew quiet. Only then did I get up and go to where the Americans were shooting.

On 25 May 1945 Johann Rankl declared in testimony taken under oath and later translated into English and included as part of exhibit 6: "Later, after I had already gone to bed, I heard shots. This lasted from about 8 P.M. until 9:30 P.M." He states that this did not concern him any further. However, the tailor Josef Liebl from Tiefenbach declared in his written testimony on 25 May 1945, which was later translated into English and included as part of exhibit 4:

A Russian named Nikolai had worked with me since mid April 1945. On Saturday, 29 April 1945 I was stopped in the street by an SS man or by an infantry soldier and asked whether the Russian Nikolai was at home. [The SS man] went with me into the apartment and took Nikolai with him. I stayed at home until I heard shots. That's when I left the house and heard civilians say that Russians were being shot.

Josef Luger, born on 13 April 1892, became the new mayor on 30 April 1945, following the American invasion. He told the Americans in his test-timony, which was later included as part of exhibit 9, that he "had heard several shots between 8 P.M. and 9:30 P.M. coming from the direction of the Hochholz Forest and was terrified, because I was quite certain that now the Russians were being shot; at the time I wasn't even thinking that that's what was happening." Gertrud Gibl seemed to have been the only person to have truly observed the crime. She said:

> Late in the evening, between 8 P.M. and 9:30 P.M. one could hear several shots from the direction of the Hochholz Forest. Shortly before 10 P.M. the SS soldiers had returned from the Hochholz Forest in Tiefenbach; three of them stayed at the Knott Inn in Tiefenbach, including one private first class and one private; I might be able to recognize these three if I saw them again. The others, however, climbed into the car immediately and were singing as they drove off.

Other eyewitnesses were less forthcoming. Most tried to keep out of the matter altogether. The former mayor of the Tiefenbach community Markus Moser testified on 25 May at 9:00 P.M., in a statement that would later be included as part of exhibit 10:

> I had been mayor of the Tiefenbach community since 1 April 1933, and remained mayor up until American troops arrived on 30 April 1945. On 29 April there was a Russian POW camp here. I myself did not reside in Tiefenbach, but instead in Graming, which is located approximately three kilometers from Tiefenbach. During the last week in April there were approximately two hundred members of the SS stationed in Graming and I myself housed six or seven SS men. These SS troops began to leave during the night of 28 to 29 April, and the last SS marching posts left Graming at about 11:30 A.M. on the morning of 29 April 1945. On the morning of 28 April I went to Passau where I spoke with the district administrator of Passau, Dr. Zagel, who lives at the Domplatz in Passau; we discussed the distribution of prisoners to several communities, since the prisoners had been left behind without any guards or food supply. The local group leader, a teacher from Tiefenbach named Kreipl who now is in American custody, came to Passau on several occasions because his elderly father lived there and also because the major party meetings took place there in Passau. This local group leader said on several occasions, while at the office, that he was afraid that when the Americans arrived and the Russians were set free they would start looting. He was a strict Nazi Party member. I am not accusing teacher Kreipl of giving the order to execute the Russians, because I don't know anything about that; I don't know if he did that. But the possibility exists

that he gave the order to the SS, via the district leadership, to have the Russians executed in Tiefenbach.

Only six of the mere forty-eight remaining prisoners survived the mass execution in the Tiefenbach Hochholz Forest.

Fritz Mattes's Savings Account Book from the Federal Post Office Bank

In April 1945, Hungarian troops along with units of the German Wehrmacht, SS, Hitler Youth groups from Austria that had been assigned to the SS, and the Salzweg Volkssturm had dug in in a forested area in the vicinity of Moos and Kießling, about three kilometers north of Passau. This essentially formed what was known as the Upper Danube Combat Group, which had been originally assembled in Freystadt (Upper Austria), plus an accompanying tank destroyer unit. A 1952 report from the Passau county police states:

> The combat group was commanded by a first lieutenant of the SS, whose name could not be determined. The battle unit took its post in Patriching on 26 April 1945. According to investigations conducted thus far, the members of the SS and HJ units were Austrian. It is likely that Hitler Youth from the former Wartegau were part of it: a savings account book from the federal post office bank was found in a rifle pit close to Kießling, in the county of Passau; it was made out to the name Fritz Mattes, an engine fitter from Simmopfeim in the county of Calw, who lived at Leo Schlageter Strasse, number 14.

After the Passau SS had retreated, Hungarian SS and their Hitler Youth arrived with the mission to kill all those who for one reason or another were about to get away with their lives. Therese Mack, a broom binder's wife from Kießling provided more precise information:

> In April 1945 units of Hungarian troops, German Wehrmacht, SS, and Hitler Youth were stationed in the forested area surrounding the towns of Kießling and Moos. The latter had been assigned to the SS units and they also included members of the Austrian Hitler Youth. . . . While the Hitler Youth were stationed in the vicinity of our house they frequently used to stop by. At that time we asked them where they came from. They told us that for the most part they were from St. Pölten and Vienna.

Matthias Mautner, a farmer from Kießling stated in his testimony from 11 September 1952: "Shortly before the invasion of the Americans I was returning to Kießling from my job in Regensburg. At that time the entire area was occupied by SS, Hungarians, and Hitler Youth. One night there must have been thirty to forty Hitler Youth staying in my barn. Soon they were ordered to dig into one-man rifle pits and take up position." Karl Reisinger, the stamp manufacturer who used to live in those days at house number 3 in the Passau suburb of Ries, which is located south of Kießling and Moos, was ordered to evacuate his apartment on 28 April 1945, "because Ries had been declared a military base. I stayed with a certain Herr Jel in Haslachhof. In those days the SS were already retreating toward Ries and the boys from the Volkssturm, who were under the command of the SS, were ordered to take up position in Patriching." In 1952 Therese Mack still remembered very well the emaciated Russians from the neighboring town of Jacking, who had been left behind by the SS.

> They were very hungry so they approached houses in the area asking for food. That's when they were picked up by SS and Hitler Youth. . . . The Hitler Youth did not let any civilians enter the forest, so that it's very unlikely that anybody witnessed the execution of the Russians. During the time when the executions supposedly were taking place, the Moos Forest was crawling with Hungarians; many of them remained in the forest for several weeks even after the American invasion. Some time thereafter, when the Hungarians had fled the forest, the Mautner family reported that there was a strong smell of decay emanating from the forest. Even though people kept talking about the fact that there had to be a Russian mass grave in the forest, a search was never conducted. And no bodies were ever discovered there by chance, either. I myself did hear it said repeatedly that there allegedly was a Russian grave in the Moos Forest, but I never managed to come across anything. Sometime after the Hitler Youth were taken to a POW camp by the Americans I found several items not far from our property; in addition to equipment and weapons I also found a savings book from the federal post office bank. I took it home with me and kept it in a safe place, thinking that I might be able to send it back to the owner one day.

Getting a Look at the Murderers

The shoemaker Josef Peschl from Haselbach lived in Moos in those days; his house was located at number 84 1/3, exactly across from the crime scene. He was looking out one of his windows and from there witnessed the crime with his own eyes. In 1952 he reported very openly:

I had been living in Moos since 1928. I was at home throughout the war. During the last days of the war, Hungarian troops and Hitler Youth—in addition to the SS—were stationed the towns of Patriching, Kießling, and Moos. These units were in charge of securing the train tracks and the train crossing between the forester's house in Patriching and the town of Patriching itself; the tracks ran between Passau and Tiefenbach, that is, through the Moos Forest. I cannot exactly recall today whether this happened a few days of perhaps even a week before the Americans marched in. From my house I noticed that a group of about ten to twelve people were led into the Moos Forest, approximately 150 meters in the distance. I clearly recognized this transport as being Russian POWs. Some of the prisoners were carrying shovels. The crew escorting them consisted of members of the SS, in my estimation. They were rather tall, even taller than most of the Russian POWs. I'm certain they were not members of the Hitler Youth. But I do not rule out the possibility that there may have been Hitler Youth among them, perhaps walking ahead of the group. When asked at what time of the day I made this observation I cannot remember any specific time. I only know for certain that it was daytime. A short time after the POWs were led into the Moos Forest one could hear several shots in quick succession. I immediately thought that the POWs were being done in. The fact that they were most certainly Russian POWs was evident from their torn and mismatched clothing. The railway clerk Josef Schmöller, who at that time still lived at the farm belonging to Matthias Mautner of Kießling, told me several days later, after the Americans had already passed through, that there was a Russian grave located in a ravine in the Moos Forest. I was curious and went to take a look at the location that was pointed out to me. I found a spot covered with a thin layer of twigs. I moved the twigs out of the way and saw a foot sticking out of the ground, about up to the knee. As far as I can recall there was a wooden shoe on the foot. After that I was certain that it was the Russian POWs who had been shot and buried here.

Karl Reisinger, too, was directly confronted with the murders:

A young member of the Volkssturm told me that POWs were being shot in the Moos Forest. The executions were carried out by members of the Volkssturm. These boys were very drunk that day. The fellow who told me about it continued and said that the whole thing was an awful mess because the dead Russians weren't even properly buried and that their feet were still sticking out of the ground. It must have been around 1:30 P.M. when he told me this. Shortly afterwards the Americans marched in from the direction of Tittling. On the morning of the same day a captured Russian soldier came up to me begging for bread. My wife gave him some. At noon he reappeared asking for more. This Russian was very emaciated and completely exhausted. I saw him again some time later, accompanied by an American captain.

Fear of Getting Involved

Most of the residents were desperate not to notice anything and so to "stay out" of the whole affair. Matthias Mautner's statement is typical of this attitude:

> I did not see any Russian POWs around in those days. I have no knowledge about Russian POWs having been led into the Moos Forest and shot there. Only later did I hear about the existence of a Russian grave in the Moos Forest when Lichtenegger brought it up. Even though we noticed a strong odor [coming from the forest], I cannot say that I knew it was the odor of decaying corpses. There was just one time when our landlord, Josef Schmöller, who lives in Passau today, said that at one point he was aware of a strong odor of decay as he walked through the forest on his way to work. He kicked around in the dirt a bit with his foot and noticed a shoe sticking out of the ground. I did not concern myself with this issue and never went to see the spot where this shoe was allegedly sticking out.

Josef Peschl later admitted as well:

> Sometime later, I can't exactly remember when, I told Erwin Weber from Jägerreuth about my discovery. I did not tell anybody else about it. I did not inform the police because I was afraid that I would be ordered to assist with the exhumations. I had already been ordered to do such work once before and I had refused to do it then. This case involved the exhumation of three Russian POWs who were shot on the Geier property in Moos on the day of the shootings in the Moos Forest. Since the executions in the Moos Forest and the Geier property took place on the same day and in quick succession, I believe that the people shot on the Geier property had attempted to save themselves by escaping from the forest.

Years Later: Corpses Discovered in the Forest

Sophie Hetterich and her daughter Elisabeth were the first ones to discover the remains of the corpses in the Moos Forest while gathering wood one day in August 1947. They discussed their find with Josef Peschl and reported it to the American military government. However, this did not generate much interest among the Americans, as the CIC had closed the investigations in early 1946. The issue was taken up again only in September 1952, in Passau: a truck driver by the name of Josef Lichtenegger from Neureuth had found shoes made of leather and wood in the same forest. On 9 September 1952 the county police in Hals reported about Josef Lichtenegger's finding skeletons in Moos. The report was recorded as transcript number 1127/52 and was later sent to the senior state prosecutor. Two days later, Oberkommissar Kienberger and Kommissar Eckl from an outpost of the county police for crimes in Lower Bavaria/Upper Palatinate interviewed him. Lichtenegger stated:

> Approximately one year ago I found out through word of mouth that a Russian grave supposedly existed in the Moos Forest. Even though I was interested in this I wasn't able to find out the exact location of the grave. Then I was committed to the hospital in Passau for some time and therefore could not continue searching for the so-called Russian grave. About fourteen days later I again asked about the grave, at which time I heard that a man in Moos by the name of Peschl knew more details about the Russian grave. One Saturday afternoon I paid him a visit and asked him what he knew about it. Peschl told me that he knew where the grave was, but that he couldn't show it to me because otherwise he'd get in trouble with the police and that he wanted to have nothing to do with the affair. When I insisted, he finally agreed to show me the grave. Together we went into the state forest in the vicinity of Kießling and arrived at a large recess in the ground, which Peschl pointed out to me as the grave. During the course of our conversation and before we entered the forest, Peschl had told me that he had not been involved in burying the dead, and that instead he had hidden out in order not to be required help with this work. When we arrived at the supposed grave site I walked down into the recess in the ground and saw leather and wooden shoes lying there. When I lifted them up, toe and ankle bones fell out of the shoes. Inside one shoe there was still a woolen sock. As I lifted it up, toe bones dropped out of it onto the ground. There was even a shin bone and a leg bone stuck in there. This discovery was proof to me that this most certainly was a grave. I immediately reported my discovery to the district administration office in Passau.

Josef Lichtenegger talked with Frau Mack and found out that the Hitler Youth had "thrown away everything as the Americans were approaching."

Among the discarded items Frau Mack had found a savings account book from the federal post office bank made out in the name of Mattes Jmoppheim, from the district of Calv [Kalv], I think. She had kept this book until that day and handed it over to me upon request. But when Oberkommissar Kienberger and Kommissar Eckl had interviewed her on 11 September 1952, Therese Mack claimed to have been with her children in Schlott, in the Tiefenbach community, during the time in question. Today I found out from Frau Peschl that the railway clerk Schmöller, who used to live on the Mautner property in Kießling, had covered up the Russian grave with some underbrush because the corpses had emitted a strong odor of decay. Allegedly Peschl had himself found out from Schmöller about the existence of the grave. Schmöller is said to live in Passau today. When Peschl led me to the grave I took photographs and wanted to have them printed as proof of the existence of the grave. I had the film developed at the Hochleitner photo lab in Passau. However, the pictures didn't turn out. On Monday I took pictures of the grave yet again, in the presence of Sergeant Strohmayer of the federal police station in Hals. I handed both rolls of film over to the police station. It is my opinion that the residents in the vicinity of the grave were silent about the existence of the grave only because they were afraid that they would be ordered to perform the exhumations.

Bodies Were Piled Up Everywhere

In September 1952 a three person judicial commission and eleven others met at the grave site to begin the process of exhumation. They discovered: "Eight shattered skulls, ten sets of pelvic bones, eight pairs of arms, ten pairs of lower legs, ten pairs of lower legs and numerous other skeletal remains." The report from the Passau judicial commission further states:

> In addition numerous other skeletal remains were identified. The parts were wrapped in brown shredded uniforms that still bore partial yellow lettering. Three skulls displayed hole-like punctures, which very likely were the result of gunshot wounds. Two of these skulls showed round punctures in the back of the head; another skull shows a puncture at the left temple. The skull perforated at the back of the head also has a hole to the middle of the right skullcap. The holes have a diameter of about one centimeter. All skull bones were shattered. Judging from the position of the skeletal remains the corpses were piled up inside the pit, facing the ground. It cannot be determined from the position of the

remains with any certainty whether the corpses were thrown into the pit or whether the persons in question were shot into the pit. Consistent with the skeletal remains, ten pairs of shoes, mostly with wooden soles, were found inside the pit. From the pieces of clothing to the kind of footwear, from the remaining lettering on the uniforms—in three instances clothing displayed the yellow S.U. [Soviet Union] symbol—to the articles of clothing and cooking or eating utensils, it can be concluded that the bodies discovered were POWs. Judging from the condition of the skeletal remains it can be concluded that they had been buried in the ground for approximately five to ten years. The skeletons were covered with stones, gravel, and underbrush to a depth of thirty to fifty centimeters, and were partially overgrown with the exposed roots of some trees growing in the area. Further spot checks in the gravel pit did not result in further evidence that would determine the location of additional human remains. Beginning of excavation: 10:00 A.M.; end of excavation: 12:00 noon. Permission of release of the findings was granted to the mayor of the community of Tiefenbach.

Nothing to Be Recovered

In the "supplementary report" of 5 October 1952, the following attachments were added, which as of today have been declared "unrecoverable": "Five interrogation reports, one sketch, one illustration, one billing statement, one savings account book from the federal post office bank, one carton containing three human skulls." Furthermore it states:

It has not been possible, from this vantage point, to examine to what extent Mattes was complicit in the execution of the Russian POWs. The determination regarding perpetrators has equally not resulted in any findings so far. It is assumed that the perpetrators are at this point to be found in Austria, as the Upper Danube Combat Group was comprised of members of the SS and Hitler Youth units from Austria. . . . The weapon with which the wounds were inflicted may no longer be identified today, which is why the evidence was never submitted to the central administration in Munich. Certain papers were found in the uniforms of the executed. These were secured and sent to the central administration in Munich for the purposes of generating a statement regarding names, etc.

In November 1952, the Central Administration for Criminal Identification and Police Statistics of the State of Bavaria delivered the following statement:

Envelope number 1 contained scraps of paper that were severely soaked through with the corpse's bodily fluids and fungal growth. After drying out the leaves of paper, a successful separation of the documents could be accomplished. They mostly turned out to be documents in relation to the former railway of the Reich. Envelope number 2 contained two pieces of paper that were entirely stuck together. In order to divide these pieces of paper from each other, a mixture of diluted peroxide was applied to them in the appropriate doses so that bubbles from the released oxygen served to separate the leaves. A fluorescent photograph was taken—see attachment—which clearly shows the following:

(a) a personal identity card for POWs with the following characteristics:

LAST NAME: KALININ;   FIRST NAME: ALEXANDER;
NATIONALITY: USSR, RUSSIAN;   PROFESSION: FARMER.

(b) a pay stub or canteen receipt. This also is marked with the above mentioned personal information and the number of the personal identification card.

On 28 July 1953, the criminal procedure 7 Js 178/53 bearing the charge of "manslaughter of Russian POWs in the state forest Moos, community of Tiefenbach" was dropped by senior public prosecutor Dr. Weiss. In April 1964 the district attorney's office inquired "as to what was supposed to happen with the skulls." Dr. Welzmüller, the new public prosecutor responded:

> Return to business office. As the act was committed in the year 1945, and the statute of limitations was disrupted as a result of an arrest warrant against the perpetrators, place of residence unknown, it is recommended that the three skulls be stored as long as the statute of limitation of twenty years, which is set to expire after the final decision of the courts (and which very likely is identical with the date of issue of the arrest warrant) is still valid. Passau, 15 April 1964; signed: Senior District Attorney at the District Court Passau, Dr. Welzmüller.

The photographs that Josef Lichtenegger took of the corpses were not preserved, according to statements of the police and the district attorney's office. The remains were initially buried in a mass grave at the Tiefenbach cemetery and later transferred to Neumarkt in the Upper Palatinate. Today, the mass grave in Kießling and the graves on the Geier property are overgrown with dense forest; a gravel path belonging to the forest administration runs alongside the mass grave. Former residents say that the path was constructed right on top of the former grave. A small chapel dedicated to the Virgin Mary is located several meters from the scene of the crime, which, however, has no relation whatsoever to the murders, but instead serves as a memorial to a German soldier who died during the Second World War.

The Mass Murder on the Ries: Shot Like Rabbits

The section of forest in the Passau suburb of Ries, at the "5 kilometer" mark, is referred to in the vernacular as "Dead Man's Wood." The Hitler Youth in particular committed brutal and random murders there during the last days of the war. The victims were fatally ill and emaciated Russian POWs who were too weak even for the SS to victimize. "Everywhere in the forest there were fresh heaps of earth, holes, and pits. Frequently one could not even distinguish whether these were graves or tank tracks. Grenades and spent shell casings—and mess kits—littered the ground. We didn't dare go too deep into the forest. There were dead bodies in there; it was so horrible," a female resident remembers today. District court councilman Dr. Reitberger officially informed the Passau district attorney Stögmayer:

In my former capacity as provisional district administrator of Passau I was told in May 1945 that at the 5 kilometer mark [at Ries] several Russians had been hastily buried in the forest. Following orders issued by the former governor I inspected several corpses and determined that they were superficially buried in the ground only about twenty to thirty centimeters deep. As far as I recall, former Head Commissioner Rödl was with me then. I arranged for a search of the area for other potential corpses and ordered that they be properly and honorably buried. The residents who were interrogated claimed, so I was told, that the murderers had been uniformed young men, most likely from Austria. I was not informed whether the police were able to determine the names of the people responsible. It is to be assumed that Head Commissioners Birnberger and Sexlinger are aware of the facts in this matter. I personally did not conduct any inquires or interrogations regarding this matter at the time, due to my other responsibilities, but I remember with reasonable certainty having been informed that these Russians were "shot like rabbits." In my opinion the killings of these defenseless prisoners bear no relationship whatsoever to the events of the war. I believe that initially there were thirty-seven Russian victims, and later there were additional ones. I asked the county police to do everything in their professional power to find the perpetrators.

The county police, however, apparently found nothing.

The XX Corps of the 3rd U.S. Army arrested several of the perpetrators just a few days after the end of the war in a forested area close to the town of Ried im Innkreis and stated that they had still been "armed and hostile." They were incarcerated at a POW camp. Franz Mitterhauser was shot while attempting to escape. Erwin Engelputzeder made the following confession:

> In early April 1945 I was called up to join the Volkssturm, and on 19 April 1945 I was brought to Passau. A few days later we were transferred to our positions in Ries, in Bavaria. We were assigned to defend against approaching tanks. We finished with this job when our company leader, whose name I don't know (he was the head of the agricultural school in Otterbach), ordered us to take into custody all individuals approaching our positions. We were ordered to shoot anyone who didn't stop. Late one afternoon, I don't recall the exact date, Frank Mitterhauser, who was part of my group and who I believe lives in Stelzen, brought in a Russian POW. The company leader ordered Mitterhauser and me to take him [the prisoner] into the forest and shoot him. As I knew from previous cases, each Russian was forced to dig his own grave before he was shot. I gave him a spade and communicated to him that he had to dig his grave. When he refused, Mitterhauser and Brosen (I don't know his first name) dug a small pit. From a distance of approximately ten meters I fired the first shot into the Russian, from my own rifle, and the bullet hit him exactly below the right lung. Right after me Mitterhauser shot him and he collapsed. Mitterhauser shot him again and Brosen shot him in the neck with his revolver, which he was carrying with him. Because the hole he had dug was too small, Mitterhauser and Brosen squeezed the body together to make it take up less room and stomped on it with their boots. I was so horrified by this that I was not able to go near the spot. Mitterhauser then covered up the hole. As far as I know there were about twenty Russians who were killed in this way by our unit. I cannot name exact names [of the perpetrators], because I don't know them. As to the question of why? I did it because it was an order and I didn't want to get punished for refusing to follow an order.

Buried Alive

Shortly after the war, Princess Tatjana Kudaschew, a painter and mosaic artist born in St. Petersburg was assigned a room, together with seven other Russian emigrants, at the house belonging to the Muttenhammer family in the community of Ruderting, just a few kilometers north of

Tiefenbach. Approximately eight days after the American invasion she watched from her balcony as several Russians were talking excitedly to each other in the yard below. An emaciated Russian POW talked about how twelve of his comrades were shot at and then "thrown into a pit while still alive." After two of the emigrants managed to calm him down he told them about the events in the Tiefenbach camp. They all were outraged about the conduct of the SS. Nevertheless, it was not until 16 February 1949 that Landgerichtsrat Dr. Reitberger in Deggendorf followed up on a telephone conversation from two days before, sending Princess Kudaschew's statement to state prosecutor Stögmayer in Passau. Under point three she added that, in early January 1946, the CIC had contacted her about these crimes. The county police of Ruderting recorded the Lady's testimony in the fall of 1952, that is, some seven years later. At that time Tatjana Kudaschew was no longer able to name the exact location of the scene of the crime. But most likely she was referring to the location "Dead Man's Wood" in the Passau suburb of Ries. Tatjana Kudaschew moved to Passau in 1954 and died there in 1972 single and stateless. Nothing further about her life or the circumstances of her emigration is known today. Today anyone who finds himself standing at the location of the 5 kilometer mark at Ries is generally not there to see the place where the Russians were murdered. They most likely are waiting for the public bus: the city administration built a bus station right at the scene of the crime.

The End of the Terror

Katharina Lindner from Tiefenbach wrote the following passage in her diary:

> On Monday, 30 April, at 11:30 in the morning, the Americans arrived. Herr Rankl, Herr Liebl, Herr Geier, and Herr Ludwig Roßgoderer went out to meet them and to surrender. A white flag was raised at the church steeple, and others were displayed on most of the houses. Weapons were surrendered and inspections took place. In our case the Americans behaved properly. They demanded a strict lights out period where everyone had to be quiet, but there was no quiet for us, there was the fear of what is to come.

When the Americans arrived in Jacking the innkeepers, the Knott family, were paralyzed with fear: they had forgotten to remove the large Hitler photograph that hung in their establishment. One of their sons had to carry it across the street and was ordered to smash it to pieces against a small piece of granite in the presence of the American soldiers. The relatives were afraid for the son's life. But there were Poles, Frenchmen, and Russians who vehemently shielded the Knott family and assured the Americans that they had been treated very well by the innkeepers. The late Kathie Reitinger remembered at the end of her life how relieved they were to have spent those years of terror in peace with the prisoners. They have not heard from any of the former prisoners, however, since the end of the war. The only tangible memory they have left is a photograph of the Russian woman Ludmilla, holding Kathie Reitinger's small son in her arms.

In Fatting, the fear was also palpable: when they had run out the last of the flour rations, Herr Franz Xaver Köberl went over to the Fraunhofer house in the "Old Parsonage" next door so he would not have to see any more prisoners die in the hours before the end of the war. Just when the farmer was searching for something to eat the first Americans entered the house and asked about the POW camp. They were immediately shown the way to the barn. Of the remaining guards of the camp two surrendered, and a third fled. When Herr Köberl returned home with the sack of flour he found himself confronted with the barrel of a rifle and was asked by a suspicious American soldier if he was a member of the Nazi Party. One of the Russians who witnessed the scene immediately called out in broken German: "Don't shoot! Farmer good!"

The Americans handed out chocolate, chewing gum, and tobacco to the surviving POWs. The Russians shared their cigarettes with farmer Köberl, who always told them that if his sons were abused in this way he would have rather wished for them a quick death. Shortly after the end of the war two of farmer Köberl's sons returned from the Russian front, but they both died within seven weeks from injuries sustained during the war. In the barn next to the pig trough one can still see the tree trunk that used to hold up the straw-covered, wooden boards on which the Russians used to sleep. Köberl Jr. did not want a picture of his parents published. He thought that his father would not have agreed to it. In his words, his father was "just trying to do what he could to help out . . . as one is taught to do where one finds misery." Köberl Jr. has since died as well.

Into the Arms of the Liberators

"Thank God I made it out with my life," recalled Bokow Wasilew, "but I don't know if the others were so lucky. For two days I was living in the forest; then I went fo Lefenbach, where I saw American soldiers. They took me in and treated me well." Ivan Ivanovich Savelyeu gave his written testimony on 24 May 1945. Corporal Michael S. Drohn provided the translation into English, which was later included as part of exhibit 5. Savelyeu, who escaped from the Tiefenbach forest, remembered:

> At four o'clock in the afternoon on 30 April, Americans found me and asked me why I was naked and why I had no shoes and what I was doing standing there shivering. I tried to explain to them, but they didn't understand Russian and I didn't understand American [English]. I went to the farmers and they gave me some bread and the Americans gave me eggs; this was my first meal in two or three days. A Frenchman gave me a jacket and shoes and after that I returned to Tiefenbach and there people told me how the rest of the prisoners had been executed that day.

Reluctant Gravediggers

The murdered Russians were discovered buried approximately thirty to forty centimeters deep in a water drainage ditch close to a sewage plant. All the men from Tiefenbach between the ages of sixteen and sixty were forced by the Americans to dig up the corpses. The tailor Josef Liebl was one of them: "One of the corpses . . . I recognized as a former worker of mine [Nikolai]. The back of his head revealed a gunshot wound. I recognized him from his pants and his shirt, which I had given to Nikolai; I also recognized his face and his red hair." Almost all the dead lay in the grave one beside the other, except for the few who had attempted to flee. Katharina Lindner noted:

> A sad chapter now follows: the burial of the Russians. The townsmen had to dig a grave twenty-five meters in length at the Schinderwiese; then Herr Schwaiberger and Herr Pretzer were ordered to make the coffins. Father drove them out to the spot and then all women and girls, etc., were forced to look at the executed Russians; I asked to be allowed to remain at home and was given permission to do so. It was a horrific sight. Alois Kampfhammer and Josef Liebl laid the Russians into their coffins; then they were taken to the mass grave. The teacher Herr Kreipl was dragged into the village from the mass grave and mistreated by several enraged Russians. The Americans then gave him protection and he was taken away in an American car; may God grant his safe return.

To this day many citizens of Tiefenbach still see it as a gross injustice that the entire population of the town was forced to look at the dead.

The Occupiers Withdraw

Katharina Lindner was relieved, when:

> On Friday afternoon [3 May 1945], the Americans withdrew and our people were able to move back into their badly damaged houses; anyone who didn't move fast enough had Russians and Poles break in and steal everything. On Friday, refugees from far away began returning but found that a family of eight Russians had moved into their apartment at the schoolhouse; as a result these people from Breslau are forced to sleep and cook here at our house. Life is hard on Father; yesterday morning he had to fetch some boards from the sawmill, and in the evening he had to pick up the dead Russians—one of them was at the fire station and two he had to pick up in Jacking—drive them to the sports field and take them to the freshly dug graves there. And so it continues; the Americans haven't returned to this day. All of our meadows and fields from here all the way to Kogl are ruined; all the wheat, potato fields, oats, and barley, all of the meadows; it brings tears to one's eyes. Even in the center of the field belonging to the church, where the grain once stood high, everything is destroyed. This afternoon (we are allowed to leave our houses between 4 and 6 o'clock) I will go have a look at it myself.

Wintergreen—The Cheapest Upkeep of the Graves

As of 11 May 1945 thirty-seven Russians lived at the schoolhouse in Tiefenbach, which also served as a military hospital. A total of forty-five Russians were in Jacking and thirty-nine were in Fatting. Two weeks later the mayor of Tiefenbach informed the Passau dairy cooperative that Tiefenbach was more than one hundred percent overpopulated. Approximately eighty Russians were living in two camps and another eighty were living with individual farmers, and forty to forty-five Russians were living at the military hospital. The Russians and other foreigners needed milk and lard. The mayor complained: "They don't have to work at all . . . any more, and instead we have to treat them like guests and they're already making special demands. . . . In addition there is the nuisance of foreigners and other convoys moving through."

The Americans made sure that the Russian graves were adequately landscaped and cared for. The wintergreen plant was the cheapest ground-cover available for this purpose. It did not have to be cultivated, watered, or fertilized. It does not grow higher than a few centimeters and prevents the growth of weeds. It survives in temperatures of minus twenty degrees centigrade without any problem. Poor women have been using wintergreen for generations to decorate the graves of their relatives. The Tiefenbach community used it to decorate the graves of the murdered Russians.

On 22 May a U.S. delegation arrived in Tiefenbach to question witnesses in connection to the Russian murders. Captain Kenneth R. Wilson of the 3rd U.S. Army initially questioned the four survivors of the massacre in the Hochholz Forest, while Joseph Sabolesky quickly translated the affidavits, which were written in Cyrillic, into English. Afterwards several Tiefenbach residents were called as witnesses. Several days later the first group of surviving Russians was taken away. Where they were being sent nobody to this day remembers. The remaining ones continued to be seen as a burden. At the end of June the mayor of Tiefenbach, Herr Pfaffinger, wrote to the Passau district administrator and to the forestry administration, reporting that, due to the occupation and the numerous Russians, a significant portion of the firewood supply reserved for the winter had already been used up and asked for another cord.

On 10 October 1945 the headquarters of the 3rd U.S. Army and the Eastern Military District sent a report marked "confidential" to the War Crimes Branch, addressing the results of the inquest:

1. Initially it was pointed out that the inquest was conducted according to the guidelines of 24 February 1945; Captain Kenneth R. Wilson of the infantry and Patrick W. McMahon, Second Lieutenant of the infantry, conducted the inquest between 22 May and 25 May 1945.
2. The topic of the inquest was "Murder by execution of Russian POWs in the vicinity of Tiefenbach, Germany, on 29 April 1945, by members of the German armed forces—a violation of Article II of the Geneva Convention."
3. (a) The statements of all witnesses were recorded with the consultation of an interpreter; accordingly.
    (b) All nine witness accounts are filed in alphabetic order.
4. The summary, which was very well done, stresses one thing in particular: the fact that after the murders the SS men were "singing as they drove off."
5. Their names and the addresses of their units are unknown at this point; the Russians, however, "are now buried in an acceptable

grave; it is located one kilometer from Tiefenbach; a public funeral was held in May 1945."

Item six states that the names of all SS men stationed in Passau on 29 April 1945, were entered into a most wanted list.

Item 7 contains the following closing statement: "Forty Russian prisoners of war were brutally murdered by execution on 29 April 1945 in Tiefenbach; each soldier who participated in this unscrupulous act, as well as their superiors who gave the order for this act, will be made to atone for this direct violation of Article II of the Geneva Convention and face the maximum penalty."

On 3 December 1945, Colonel B. Mickelwait sent the report to the American military government. The report was also forwarded to the Russian occupying forces, so that they could research the information or begin other appropriate procedures. In February 1946 the last Russians were deported to the Soviet Union. How many of them had been in Tiefenbach can no longer be determined; the present local administration is no longer in possession of the relevant documentation.

The Memorial

In December 1946 the mayor of Tiefenbach, Herr Pfaffinger, informed the district administration of Passau that his community had incurred expenses in the amount of fifty reichsmarks for the "landscaping, decoration, and care" of the three large Russian mass graves. Six months later he secured the services of a community worker at the gardening department, so that it could begin a project of planting fir trees. The bill was sent to the community. The preservation of war graves was at least partially financed by the State of Bavaria. But when the people of Tiefenbach asked to be reimbursed for the cost of a simple wooden cross, the district administration informed them, that "according to article 74, number 10, and article 120 of the constitution, the State of Bavaria is not responsible for the cost. . . . It is therefore doubtful whether the costs will be fully refunded."

In December 1953 the stonemason Josef Höldl from Graming, in the district of Tiefenbach, presented his design for a new memorial to be built at the Russian grave at Grubmühle: it was a stone cross of 1.65 meters in height, and made of white granite. The horizontal arm of the cross was to be one meter in length and was to bear the inscription "UNKNOWN RUSSIAN SOLDIERS." The shape of the cross was slightly reminiscent of the

Iron Cross, or Eiserne Kreuz, which was conferred upon German soldiers for special merit. In 1956 the dead were again exhumed and reburied at the cemetery in Neumarkt, in the Upper Palatinate region of Bavaria. The originally white stone cross, which by now is partially overgrown with moss, is located today to the left of the sewage plant, about fifty meters east of the path leading toward Gaißamühle. The forest there is dense and high, the trees being close to sixty years old now. There is no sign to notify visitors of the memorial, and only people familiar with the area are able to find it. "THIS IS THE FINAL RESTING PLACE OF RUSSIAN SOLDIERS," the inscription still (falsely) reads on the horizontal arm of the cross. The wintergreen that was planted there over half a century ago still marks the spot where on 29 April 1945, at least forty Russian soldiers were brutally slaughtered by the SS.

Forty Years Later: A Service at the Memorial

For many years the Motor Yacht Club (MYC) of Passau has enjoyed amicable relations with the ship owners of neighboring nations. In 1985 the captain of the Soviet passenger ship "Dnjepr" invited members of the MYC to a party on his boat. They talked about the end of the war, and the tax advisor Walter Stadler mentioned the Russian grave in Tiefenbach. A delegation of the "Dnjepr" was planning to use the last Danube cruise of the year to visit the memorial, accompanied by the Soviet embassy councilor. Members of the MYC helped arrange the event.

A wreath was to be laid, and "a handshake across the graves" was planned as a gesture to fortify a mutual friendship. But almost nobody in Tiefenbach was truly enthusiastic about this private attempt to come to terms with the past. The councilmen of Tiefenbach were vehemently against the plan that their mayor should participate in the wreath-laying ceremony. "Why open up old wounds?" they insisted. In order for the Soviets to even be able to travel outside the Passau city limits, they were required to have an official permit. This was granted: "On the basis of the occasion of the wreath-laying ceremony on 27 November 1985, between 11 A.M. and 5 P.M."

Thirty-eight guests from the Ukraine drove through the deeply snowed-in forest in two small buses. The roads were icy, and there was no sign to point out the memorial. The people had to tramp fifty meters through the thick forest and then lay down the large wreath made from fir branches and decorated with a red poinsettia. The band was inscribed in Cyrillic letters. Walter Stadler, who was accompanied by members of the MYC board Adam Golombeck and Joachim Rübenach, briefly talked about the shock expressed by the population regarding the massacre of the Russians during the final hours of the war. An interpreter was there to translate. Walter Stadler shook hands with Valentin Solowiev, the representative of the Soviet navigation on the Danube in Regensburg. Solowiev thanked Stadler for the friendly reception. And Captain Boris Mascharow commented that events such as this must never be repeated, and that everyone should live in peace.

Afterwards the group visited a farmer whose father-in-law had saved the lives of five Russians. The community sent out a snowplow to clear the way leading through the forest, as otherwise the icy road would have been inaccessible. The farmer was waiting for the group, and pointed out to the Soviets the exact spot where their fellow countrymen had survived. He told how, at the time, his father-in-law, Hans Scholler, had hurriedly emptied the cesspool, hiding the prisoners there for four days and providing them with food. The entrance to this hiding place can be seen to this day. The Soviet visitors passed around a photograph of Scholler and were told that only in 1956 had his brother-in-law finally returned home from a Russian prison camp. Afterwards they toured the farm; at this point Ludwig Rankl, the mayor of Tiefenbach, and his deputy mayor were suddenly also on hand to join the tour. Then they all went to dinner together at the nearby Grubmühle Inn, where they drank wheat beer and vodka. Ludwig Rankl presented the captain of the "Dnjepr" with a coat of arms of the Tiefenbach community and received a gift in return. The atmosphere might have been less cheerful had the Russian guests been aware of the fact that in 1945 (according to statements made under oath) Rankl, as a member of the Hitler Youth, had been involved in the shooting of Russian POWs. Moreover, the innkeeper of the Grubmühle, who happened to be Rankl's brother, himself had good reason not to talk about "back then." He knew very well what had happened to the Russian POWs in Tiefenbach, in 1945. A highly embarrassing incident was barely avoided: because the Soviet delegation had left city limits during its visit and thus entered the county itself, the border police filed a report of breach of the terms of their visitation visa. But this went too far even for the Passau senior public prosecutor—he had the proceedings closed quickly and secretly.

CHAPTER 4

Pocking Waldstadt

Driving in the direction of Passau on the B 12 federal highway one passes, shortly after the Pocking exit, the concentration camp memorial site of Pocking-Waldstadt. It is well hidden behind a dense growth of tall trees. A tiny green sign with three crosses marks the entrance. At the end of the Second World War, concentration camp prisoners were raped, tortured, and murdered here. After the end of Nazi rule, the town became home to the largest Jewish community in Germany, with over 10,000 members.

Even locals have difficulty slowing their cars down in time to navigate the hairpin curve in the road that leads to the memorial. Traffic is frequently so busy that turning off there makes a collision seem nearly unavoidable. Anyone who dares to proceed will at first see only tall trees. They are for the most part German oak trees, planted just before the Second World War. In an interview from 25 May 1992, in Osterholzen, Georg Osterholzer, who served as county councilman for twenty-five years and deputy district administrator of Griesbach for another ten years, remembered how it all began in Pocking-Waldstadt:

> In 1936/37 Hitler began to expand the Wehrmacht. Stephan Valentin Bühl was mayor of Pocking at that time. He brought the Wehrmacht here. We were all expropriated and received seven hundred reichmarks per acre for our land. It was scandalous. But there was nothing we could do about it. At the end of '36 they began building the airport. Alternate airports were set up in the neighboring villages of Mittich and Kirchham. The actual airport, though, was in Pocking-Waldstadt. The Nazis needed the airports to quickly move in and claim Austria and Czechoslovakia. I remember it very well: the bombs had already arrived there two years earlier; they were stored outside, just barely concealed; the

area was guarded so nobody could get to them. When the time came [to start military maneuvers] they issued the order for one thousand beds to be built immediately! All the carpenters, everybody worked on them. To make one thousand beds overnight wasn't easy. They had to be installed at the Alter Horst, an old air hangar. Every pilot was to have his own bed. The evening before the invasion of Austria all the pilots were already there. Planes were everywhere. Before the invasion of Czechoslovakia it was the same story. No, we weren't surprised [that Germany was invading]; obviously the whole thing had been planned long ago. More and more soldiers moved in; in the end there were six thousand of them. The colonel had the Kirchham Forest cut down and the barracks built from the wood from the felled trees. Those bastards. Almost one thousand barracks were built. They didn't care who owned the forest. They weren't interested. Altogether there were ten training companies. Menzel from Pocking was an instructor there. He was training people.

Buried in a Hurry: The Gravel Pit

The former mayor of Pocking Stephan Valentin Bühl explained years later during an interrogation, which is documented in a 19 December 1950 affidavit:

A V2 rocket launching site was supposed to be built in the area of the reserve airfield in Kirchham; a department of the Wehrmacht was in charge of the job. The engineering department of the Luftwaffe did not oversee the task. Instead, the Andorfer Company was commissioned with the building project; they were assigned a work command consisting of two hundred prisoners . . . from the Flossenbürg concentration camp.

The actual number of concentration camp prisoners used for the purpose was most likely twice as high; Franz Denk, the owner of a construction company from Passau, was brought in on the project. It was a known fact that Denk had several hundred slave laborers, including women and children, in the occupied Eastern territories working for him. Denk had a reputation as a profiteer of the Nazi regime; during his inquest after the war, however, he was only charged with "minor incriminations." This puzzled many, especially since, in addition to his role as Scharführer (Nazi squadron leader) and member of the SA, Denk had been a founding member of the SS as early as 1933. During his inquest he repeatedly stated that his only

activity in the SA was limited to his hobby involving carrier pigeons. Former slave laborers confirmed having been treated decently by Denk.

According to the 12 March 1943 issue of the *PNP,* approximately four
hundred prisoners arrived in Pocking on foot. Most of them were political prisoners, and many of them had been very badly treated and were
close to death. According to the 13 April 1947 article from page three of
the *PNP* with the headline "CONCENTRATION CAMP MEMORIAL A WARN-
ING TO HUMANITY," they were people, "who in many cases had endured
the torture of imprisonment for years." A similar article found on page
three of the 12 March 1949 issue of the *PNP* bearing the headline "THE
WALDSTADT CRIMES," stated that "they were treated worse than animals."
Abraham Eiboszyc was a prisoner in the Waldstadt concentration subcamp from April 1945. He had already been in Auschwitz and after that in
Flossenbürg. The conditions in Waldstadt were the worst of any of the
camps he had been held in. There was barely any food, and there was no
medical personnel at all. In addition the prisoners were badly beaten for
no reason at all. Abraham Krotewski confirmed this, saying that Waldstadt was by far the worst camp. He noted that prisoners were frequently
beaten with such brutality that they were not able to get up again. They
were then "left to their fate," lying on their cots; several prisoners are said
to have died in this manner. In an affidavit dated 19 December 1950
Stephan Bühl made the following claim about the conditions in the camp:
"The work commando was stationed in the workers' barracks of the
flight-training school number 3; their food was prepared at the school;
their rations were equivalent to the rations of the soldiers." The *PNP*
reported in further detail about the conditions in the Pocking-Waldstadt
camp:

> One of the barracks was occupied by six SS guards, while four hundred
> political dissidents, deemed pariahs by the Nazi regime, were crammed
> into a single hut that was built to accommodate no more than forty
> people. There were no washing facilities at all. Soon there was an infes-
> tation of lice. The food supply was extremely bad, and the rest of the
> "care" was equally miserable. Within six weeks two hundred people
> were suffering from lingering illnesses and dying of hunger and mal-
> treatment.

In the abovementioned affidavit, Mayor Bühl declared that the prisoners
"had been treated by medical personnel of the Luftwaffe." When asked

again specifically, Bühl admitted that "a number of prisoners passed away at the Luftwaffe Reserve hospital in Schönburg"; but stressed that they had been "properly buried at the community cemetery Schönburg, located approximately one kilometer north of the Pocking-Waldstadt camp." The *PNP*, however, reported the following in the article "The Waldstadt Crimes": "The dead were quickly covered with earth, just like dead animals, in a nearby gravel pit." The only reliable and more complete source of information is to be found in the notes taken by Rabbi Meisels; he recalled, among other things, how

> fifty men were buried in the sand pit on the road from Schönburg to Pocking; twenty-five at the Schönburg cemetery; another twenty-one in a field beside the road from Schönburg to Kirchham, about two hundred meters from the church. One hundred additional corpses could no longer be found, exhumed, or transferred in early 1945. They lie scattered in the neighboring surroundings. And it was only after the liberation of the forced laborers by American troops on 2 May 1945 that the victims finally received a proper burial.

At his 19 December 1950 interrogation Stephan Bühl further claimed:

> Around the beginning of April 1945 two prisoners came up to me at the municipal office and requested the loan of certain tools to bury a dead comrade. They then rejected my offer to assign them a grave in our community cemetery, with the explanation that they already had a grave site close to the air base . . . and that they would bury the corpse there. This was the one and only encounter I had with these concentration camp prisoners.

Mayor Bühl's interest in these encounters does not seem to have been too great. When asked he stated that only once had he "inquired, at the occasion of an official meeting with the commander of the flight-training school regarding information about this work command." He apparently was satisfied with the explanation that the Luftwaffe had "nothing to do with it." The incidents of death simply occurred due to the fact that "the prisoners had already arrived completely undernourished and sick." The mayor responded: "We have no knowledge about mistreatment or infringement by the guard personnel and it is unlikely that any such thing occurred. It is certain that not a single case involving the Kapos went to court in Dachau." However, according to his own statements "more than a thousand civilians and employees" were working at the airbase at the time. And according to a statement by the former prisoner Abraham

Eiboszyc, they had full access to the otherwise "closely guarded construction sites" and were in daily contact with the prisoners. He never asked the employees about their experiences in the camp.

In issue 93 from 1946 the *PNP*, its contents still being closely watched by both the Americans and the few Jewish survivors, published a report on page five about the Pocking concentration camp with the headline "REMEMBERING THE POCKING CONCENTRATION CAMP," with a special focus on the barracks. They allegedly were "filthy and infested with vermin. Four hundred prisoners from fourteen different countries, with different religious backgrounds had been given only turnips that were originally intended as animal feed to eat and thus eventually were nearly starved to death." The report continues: "In the early morning hours they were driven out toward the airport on foot, with insults and beatings inflicted upon them by a brutal guard crew, in order to build defense installations for a useless war. Famished and exhausted they returned to the barracks at night, where they were simply left to vegetate, crowded together within cramped quarters."

Georg Osterholzer, in the 25 May 1992 interview, remembered exactly how this took place:

> The prisoners were in bad shape. We could see that. They had almost nothing to eat. They were so starved that people lined up to throw some bread in the streets for them. When the prisoners walked by we ran away. Their guards were mean and nasty. They beat the prisoners with sticks if they tried to pick up a few morsels. They tried to wolf down the food as fast as they could, because they were all starving. My siblings remember this even better than I do. I was fighting in the war and was only there on leave. We had several pear trees of mediocre quality growing close to the street, and when we saw the group of prisoners approach we climbed into the trees and gave them a good shake. In the spring there weren't many pears left, and they didn't taste very good either; but they ate everything, all of it. And they were so badly beaten by the guards. I was a soldier for six years, trapped and surrounded in Königsberg. We were hungry then, too. I often thought to myself about how we Germans were treating the prisoners. How they had to suffer from hunger while in captivity with us.

"Ninety-five people did not survive the assignment," wrote the *PNP* in 1946. "They died of malnutrition, illness, and abuse." However, on page three of the 13 June 1947 issue of the *PNP*, the contradictory claim is made that "During the brief period approaching the end of the war, two hundred

127

prisoners died at the camp as a result of exhaustion, illness, maltreatment, or 'liquidation.'" And indeed more conflicting information is to be found in the 8 November 1990 *PNP* article with the headline "COMMEMORATING THE GRAVELESS GRAVEYARD." A quote from the 1946 issue 93 of the *PNP* describes the "unspeakable suffering in a time, when, every morning in the grey of dawn, emaciated prisoners, so-called striped-criminals, were laying to rest their comrades who had been murdered or died of starvation." The 13 June 1947 *PNP* article further stated that "in the vicinity of the former camp there was a square gravel pit, in which the remains of concentration camp prisoners who were inhumanly killed were buried." And the 8 November 1990 *PNP* article detailed how "not a word of consolation was spoken at these earthen pits, in which the bodies of the tortured were hastily buried. There was nobody to place flowers on the graves. There was only the silence of the gravediggers, who, as they looked upon the muddy ground of the pit thinking that soon it would be their turn to find their eternal rest here, finally free of their existence in a world of horror called Pocking." Georg Osterholzer said: "Only Father Magnus Huber from Reichersberg, who was the camp priest, organized a collection for the prisoners. But many of them were sick with typhus and he was infected. He died after the war."

The *PNP* reported in a retrospective report about the end of the Pocking-Waldstadt concentration subcamp:

The attacks on the airports located in Pocking and Kirchham became more and more frequent . . . while the Luftwaffe's defenses gradually decreased. Streams of emaciated Russian POWs who had come by foot from industrial areas in Upper Silesia, passing through all of Germany and Czechoslovakia on their way, were driven like cattle through the villages. They approached farmhouses, asking for bread. The priest of the village of Kirchham, in an unprecedented action, pleaded in his sermon for help for the concentration camp prisoners, who had earlier been forced to work on construction sites at the airport. The SS prohibited food distribution—which thanks to the local population was plentiful—but they could not prevent some of the farmers' wives from coming nearly every day carrying with them entire baskets filled with bread and dumplings for the prisoners. The guards, who were almost exclusively former army veterans, did not take any steps to prevent this.

As reported in the 3 May 1946 issue of the *PNP,* an eyewitness noted in his diary on 24 April 1945: "7 A.M. in Kirchham. Discipline and order have deteriorated. When the SS guards had gone, a concentration camp prisoner inquired 'Comrade, how much longer?' The discipline of the Hungarian SS men who were less than seventeen years of age, was still good," The entry for the next day read: "Frequent visits by higher officers. Drills and harassment by the SS have become fewer. Various guards have secretely asked for civilian clothes in order to escape. . . . The Neuburg Forest resembled an ant heap. There were people everywhere." Finally, as reported in the 13 June 1947 issue of the *PNP*, "on 2 May 1945, the survivors [of the Pocking concentration subcamp] were liberated by the Americans and transferred to military hospitals."

Mass Grave at the Pocking Train Station

A sign above the platform at the Pocking train station indicates: trains from and to Mühldorf. Few today realize that on 19 April 1945, shortly before the end of the Second World War, yet another tragedy took place right here. The former mayor Stephan Valentin Bühl testified five years later, on 12 January 1950, that "in the morning hours a hostile, low-flying air attack was launched against the Pocking train station." During this attack "a train, positioned on the tracks and holding eight hundred concentration camp prisoners from the Buchenwald concentration camp, was also hit." Bruno Müller, whose property lies only a few meters from the station, lived through this attack, and in a telephone interview of 22 May 1992, described the scene:

The train had been standing there no more than maybe a couple of hours. The bombs literally appeared out of thin air. Nobody knew what was happening. I ran into the house. After the attack I checked to see what had happened outside. My wife was with me and many other people were there, too. Nobody came to stop us. What we saw was horrible. Dead bodies were lying everywhere, all torn apart. They were on the tracks, on the crossings, everywhere. Torn-off body parts, only pieces left. Everything was covered in blood. The train cars themselves were ripped apart. Most likely the pilots thought they were carrying ammunition. Instead they were filled with people.

Mayor Bühl testified under oath on 12 January 1950:

When the attack was over . . . the SS guards for this particular train . . . had the dead removed from the train cars and laid out on the platform. I received a call about the incident from the director of the railway station at the time, Herr Jankowitz. I, in turn, contacted the SS guard crew

. . . via messenger. Subsequently two ranked men (most likely sergeants) showed up at the mayor's office in Pocking. . . . Since neither of the two men spoke nor understood a word of German, communication was only possible by consulting with the camp interpreter Kubiak of the VAW (United Aluminum Works); I personally had him sent for. The two SS men demanded I take care of the burial procedures for the dead. For this reason I asked them for the personal data and the roll numbers of the deceased. I was denied this information with the comment that this was exclusively the business of the guard command and the camp administration of the respective concentration camp. I replied to the SS men: "If you do not hand over the documents you will bury these dead yourself." So the dead people were left behind on the platform.

Mayor Bühl further stated:

I then had to concern myself with the corpses. I called up the supervisory board of the district administration in Griesbach, reported the matter, and was ordered for the time being to arrange for the funerals of the dead right then and there. I ordered the Russian laborers to prepare the mass grave and to bury the dead. As far as I remember, approximately fifty-six people were buried. Due to the missing documents the names of the dead persons could not be recorded at the registry office in Pocking. The registration of these people would have to be undertaken by the concentration camp administration in charge.

Josef Gaisberger, who was working at the time as a clerk in the municipal office in Pocking, remembers that the train was driven down to the Rottwerk industrial yard, a few kilometers away; he also recalled how distraught his father had seemed when he came home that night. As reported in a telephone interview of 22 May 1992, he told him: "I have never seen anything so awful. They just shot and killed several hundred wounded people there."

In a conversation on 7 July 1991, held in the Pocking cemetery, an eyewitness remembered that in the last days of the war the SS had ordered hundreds of Russian POWs to line up at the Pocking train station and had then calmly proceeded to shoot them one after the other. The train cars that had been destroyed during the air raid were unhitched, the corpses transferred to other cars and taken away. In the morning the train left from Pocking heading southwest via Simbach to Mühldorf. Josef Gaisberger, in a tlephone interview of 22 May 1992, told of how "every few meters they threw a dead body out of the moving train. They did this along the entire stretch. Every few days, another corpse was discovered. They all were dead Russians, I believe. All shot, lying right next to the tracks."

Shortly afterwards the German troops quickly fled the area of Pocking-Waldstadt. Josef Gaisberger stated:

> The German forces occupying the airports of Pocking and Kirchham moved off toward Austria after they had blown up the remaining airplanes. Before that the camp had been transferred to the Hungarians who had stayed behind. This was the signal to raid the camp. People from far and wide rushed toward the camp with handcarts, trucks, and tractors to scavenge Wehrmacht paraphernalia that were left behind; they took anything that wasn't nailed down.

The *PNP* did not report on this event; it was apparently more important to the paper to say instead that, "among the plunderers was also a large group of foreign workers as well as an occasional Russian POW. Finally Hungarian soldiers forced the crowd out of the camp at gunpoint; they were able to end the commotion only after threatening to blow up the entire camp." The reporting style of the *PNP* in those days was rather interesting. On 2 May 1945, as described on page five of the 7 May 1949 issue of the *PNP*, the first Americans arrived:

> Within minutes their car was surrounded by frantically gesticulating Hungarians. A young woman came rushing by waving a red-white-and-green [Hungarian] flag, which the soldiers kissed respectfully—the scene was rather theatrical—and several minutes later a flag displaying the Stephan's Crown [for the former king of Hungary, St. Stephen] was waving above the Waldstadt camp. Several difficult days followed. Tank fire thundered all along the Inn River, more likely for purposes of making an impression, since no major damage was reported anywhere. Former chief engineer Dirigl was able to prevent the planned detonation of the Egglfing dam at the last minute and after a short time American tanks were in control of the river crossing into Austria. In most villages German soldiers remained behind, and during the next several days they were rounded up by the GIs and led off into prison camps, unless they had preferred to don disassembled civilian clothing in an attempt to flee in the direction of their homes. The most difficult test of nerves was posed by the frequent looting, committed not by American soldiers . . . but rather by Polish foreign workers, with which the entire district was swarming—as was most of Germany. Many of them had come to take their revenge for real or imagined injustices. Many of the Russian POWs took part as well. Kirchham and Egglfing were hit particularly

hard, as were a number of other localities. However, many a farmer was saved from injury by their Eastern workers.

On 8 May, the *PNP* wrote: "An ancient prophesy has come true: the pig's snout [the name given to the area by the locals] has been spared."

In Plastic Bags to the Pocking Cemetery

In 1949 the following appeared in the *PNP:* "Only after the liberation of the slaves by the Americans were the victims properly buried on 2 May 1945." According to information provided by Bruno Müller in a telephone interview of 22 May 1991, sometime in September 1945 the Americans saw to it that a proper burial was arranged for the victims killed at the Pocking train station. According to an eyewitness, the body parts were exhumed, packed into plastic bags, and transferred to the Pocking cemetery. The grave was given the number 97; it was a mass grave. People familiar with the cemetery freely pointed out "where the Russians were." Today these three graves are empty. In December 1946 the remains of the murdered Russians were transferred once more to Pocking-Waldstadt, as part of the present memorial, close to the B 12 federal highway.

In 1960 the *PNP* also reported, if somewhat inconclusively, about the dead of the concentration subcamp: "In December 1945 the hastily buried corpses were transferred to a new graveyard along the street leading to the town of Tutting. The American military government had ordered all former NSDAP members and their families in Pocking to participate in the event, so that people may convince themselves of the cultural shame committed on the soil of our homeland." The new graveyard referred to here is most likely identical to the memorial site along the B 12 federal highway. On 21 December 1945 this cemetery was consecrated. "The American soldiers decorated the graves with flowers and enclosed the area with a simple fence," the report in the 1946 issue number 93 of the *PNP* states. "The cross dedicated to the dead bore the inscription: 'THEY WERE MURDERED—BUT THEIR SPIRIT LIVES ON.'"

The *PNP* further noted: "As the Americans were advancing, the people who had been tortured made a promise to build a memorial, marking this place of terror." The article continued: "Rabbi Meisels, of the Pocking Jewish community, himself a former prisoner of the concentration camp, made the decision to choose this gravel pit as the site to honor the memory of the murdered victims of the Pocking concentration camp. . . . This place shall serve as a warning to future generations . . . to never stray from the path of humanity."

Building the Memorial: It Took Years

Still under the watchful eyes of the Americans and Jews, the *PNP* reported in detail in issue number 93 about the process of erecting the memorial from the very beginning: "An American, with the aid of a surviving clergyman, took it upon himself to build a memorial in honor of the murdered from fourteen nations. The first stones have already been placed." The 13 June 1947 issue related the following: "Based on the ideas of Rabbi Meisels, the engineer Herr Perkal from the Jewish community undertook the management of the construction project. Members of the Jewish community, together with former concentration camp prisoners, began the general preparations on the spacious area, which measures fifty meters by eighty-three meters. Afterwards firms and artists hired for the project began their assignments."

Friedrich Appel was there at the time and claims that the Kusser Company of Hauzenberg was ordered to deliver the stones without ever having been paid for them. The company denies this. Contradictory versions are circulating regarding the assignment of tasks. Survivors of the terror claim that companies that had been found guilty during de-Nazification trials were forced to contribute materials and labor free of charge. Herr Bauer of the Kusser Company, however, states that only those companies that had been found to have been not involved were allowed to participate in the project. Both versions are untrue. The Bavarian Castles, Parks, and Lakes Administration claims in a letter dated 12 March 1992 that they "have no knowledge" with regard to the criteria for project assignment. Rabbi Meisels kept and filed each invoice. Everything was indeed paid for. It is not known who exactly received the work orders; there is also no definitive information as to the criteria for assignments. Most likely it was a simple matter in which whomever was capable of delivering what was necessary was hired and the cleared before the courts in an expedited fashion in order to allow the deal to happen—regardless of the past. Victims and perpetrators thus worked side by side, relying on each other, so that they could not afford to tolerate any animosity. One of the people who applied for the job was Andreas Capellaro from Sulzbach on the Inn. According to a statement made by the construction engineer Friedrich

Appel, he was scheduled to start work at the beginning of November 1945. But as he was still waiting for his de-Nazification trial at the time and therefore not allowed to work. Appel himself was commissioned to begin building the obelisk, which was to be seventeen meters in height, at the memorial site. An article in the *PNP* from 22 November 1990 described the construction process. The stones used by the Kusser Company of Hauzenberg, approximately forty centimeters long each, were numbered and ready. Permits to obtain all the necessary materials were on hand. But since there was a shortage of workers, progress was very slow. Friedrich Appel constructed scaffolding twenty-four meters in height in order to lift and place the heavy stones. He borrowed a cable hoist from the cathedral workshop, which was normally used to wind up the bells. Appel himself does not remember this work fondly: in 1990 he reiterated in a letter to the editor of the *PNP* that he was forced to ride his bike to work every day. Moreover it seems to have irritated him that the statistician of the Jewish Committee had claimed in the 22 November 1990 *PNP* article that "the Jewish people are going to establish their own promised land."

The building of the memorial was so slow that eventually the foundation, which housed one hundred coffins containing 150 corpses, fell into disrepair and grass was literally growing over it. Vandalism, however, was alive and well in those days. The incomplete memorial saw its first act of desecration just a few months later in 1946. Under pressure from the Jewish community, the *PNP* wrote about the event on page five of issue 93 from 1946: "Only those in the know are reminded of unbearable sufferings by these gray stones." Then they asked: "Will somebody eventually be found to complete the construction of this memorial?" In January 1947 it was reported that the district administration would assume part of the cost for constructing the memorial. A committee made up of representatives of the military government, the district administration, the mayoral office, the UNRRA (United Nations Relief and Rehabilitation Administration), the technical directors, and the survivors committed to the completion and maintenance of the memorial. The various duties were assigned. According to an article in the *PNP* from 8 January 1947, "Stonemasons, sculptors and many other craftsmen worked diligently so that the memorial could be consecrated on the anniversary of the liberation of the camp." The construction was delayed another six weeks. On 13 June 1947, the *PNP* announced that "due to the unavailability of the Bavarian

State Commissioner in charge of issues involving people per-secuted on the basis of racial, political, or religious reasons, Dr. Philip Auerbach, the opening ceremony planned for this Sunday has to be (once again) post-poned." The event finally took place on Sunday, 22 June 1947. The Bavarian State Administration of Castles, Gardens, and Lakes reported that "the costs and other details regarding the original erecting of the monument are unfortunately not known to us." Several thousand people attended the opening ceremonies at the memorial. Altogether fourteen speeches were given, in German, English, Serbo-Croatian, and Hebrew. Among the speakers were Alois Egger, a representative of the Bavarian Parliament, State Secretary Dr. Ankermüller, and the Vice President of the Bavarian Parliament, Konrad Kübler. State Commissioner Dr. Auerbach noted that "reparation was a burning issue": many people were afraid to address it at the risk of becoming unpopular. However, it would have to be addressed "by all means possible. For this purpose one had to utilize those people who had benefitted from the party or the war during the time of the Nazi regime." He harshly criticized de-Nazification in Bavaria. Up to that point the de-Nazification courts had confiscated only thirty-three million deutschmarks in penance funds. Yet during the Nazi regime the "penance funds" from Jews alone had amounted to 368 million deutschmarks.

If one stands before the memorial today one notices seven large, empty slabs of granite set into the wall itself—one in the back and three on each side of the obelisk. Originally, the names of all the known dead from the concentration camp (but not the Russians buried there) and their dates of death were recorded there. The last line had read: "AND AN ADDITIONAL 102." Stars of David and crosses were engraved above the names. The large Stars of David located just before the slabs, however, were "removed" as early as 1947. At the time, the *PNP* reported that this was a case of "grave desecration" and that "an act of sabotage" had been committed. Allegedly "the population" was "very upset" about the incident.

The Monster of Pocking

On 2 December 1947, the *PNP* reported on the former Kapo Ernst Friebe, who was sentenced to four years in work camp for the atrocities he committed. He was classified as an "organizer." The population of the entire region could read about "a thus far unique case that has come before the de-Nazification court." The case became known publically on 28 November 1947, during a trial against the gardener Ernst Friebe from the town of Hirschberg in the Riesengebirge mountains of Silesia.

In the spring of 1945, the concentration camp inmate Ernst Friebe arrived at the Pocking camp on a transport with mostly Jewish prisoners from the Flossenbürg concentration camp. Soon after he was made Kapo. He mistreated his fellow sufferers "in a most brutal manner." If the cane wasn't enough to satisfy his sadism he beat them with shovels or other tools until his victims fell to the ground unconscious and bloody. In his prosecutorial arguments the public prosecutor Nerdinger made a clear-cut case for the fact that Friebe did indeed commit these atrocities. Numerous witnesses, themselves former prisoners at the Pocking concentration camp, testified under oath about the inhuman actions of the defendant, Friebe: he was even more vicious than the SS henchmen, and was known as "the monster." On one occasion he himself was beaten by the other Kapos for his excessive brutality. One time a Russian man died as a result of the abuse he suffered at the hands of Friebe. The prosecution's case was strengthened by the defendant's demeanor; he was unable to deny or disprove any of the accusations against him. Another key was the testimony of Herr Würzinger, a priest from Kirchham, formerly from Egglfing. He declared that two days before the American invasion, Friebe showed up asking him for civilian clothes. Apparently Friebe wanted to evade responsibility and escape the wrath of former prisoners of the concentration camp who had been under his command. He successfully did so until June 1945, when he was arrested and incarcerated at the Moosburg internment camp. Although the public prosecutor "only" demanded to classify Friebe as an "instigator," he was classified as an "organizer." The primary reason for this was the "cunning of the accused as well as the fact that he already has a criminal record."

Jewish Communities in Pocking and Waldstadt

For years Anna Rosmus has searched for the remaining eyewitnesses from the Pocking Jewish community. Finally, in Israel, she was able to find Rabbi Meisels, one of the founders of this community. Shortly before his death he granted her access to his entire collection of documents from that time. In this way it became possible for the first time to describe the structure, the daily goings on, and the disintegration of the Pocking Jewish Community.

Directly after war's end, between 2,000 to 2,500 Hungarian members of the SS settled on the land where the Pocking-Waldstadt concentration camp was located. They were equestrian troops that were supposed to assist in the defense of Austria and the Passau region, as well as units that had attempted to escape the approaching Russian troops. "They all had the SS insignia branded into their skin," says Georg Osterholzer, "and would have been immediately taken prisoner by the Russians. They knew this and were afraid of being kidnaped. And the Americans had already arrived here in the Rott River valley. They preferred to deal with the Americans. They were well-off living here with us. They eventually moved away little by little. We didn't maintain any contact with them, but if there had been any instances of collaboration or any problems, I would definitely have known about it." Josef Gaisberger, who at the time was a city employee, confirms this: "The Hungarians mostly stayed for just a few months." After the Hungarians moved away, one of the largest Jewish communities within bombed-out, postwar Germany was established in Pocking-Waldstadt. The so-called displaced persons camps were built immediately after the end of the war as a result of the liberation of the concentration camps. The term "displaced person," or DP, was introduced by the UNRRA and the military government. It was used as a designation for people who had been displaced from their home countries by the Nazis and taken (usually) to Germany and Austria. Of the nearly eight million DPs in Europe by the end of the war, about 50,000 were Jews, primarily from Eastern Europe. But while most DPs were quickly repatriated, most of these "Eastern Jews" did not want to return and soon asked instead for permission to immigrate to Palestine.

The majority of Jewish DPs lived in the American-occupied zone; there they established their own camps and centers, including one in Pocking-Waldstadt. Confronted with the chaos that followed the war, and without a secure future ahead of them, the DPs had to find a way to organize in order to survive. For many it was simply unbearable to continue living in the land of their executioners. And the German population was not able to cope, as the existence of such camps reminded them of events they were trying as quickly as possible to forget.

Up until 1947 the UNRRA was in charge of the administration for the DPs. In 1947 the IRO (International Refugee Organization) took over this task. The American Joint Distribution Committee, the Jewish Agency, the World Jewish Congress, and the ORT organization (a vocational training organization) took over the responsibility for maintaining the Jewish DP camps and helped with emigration procedures. The establishment of the State of Israel in May 1948 came as a tremendous relief to many of the Jewish DPs. By 1951 the majority of Jews had emigrated to Palestine. The last DP camp was dissolved in 1953.

Establishing the Community

The *PNP* printed the following on the establishment of the Pocking Jewish community.

> The basis . . . for the community was established by Rabbi Leopold Meisels shortly after liberation. Dressed in prisoner's clothes and wearing wooden shoes, the former prisoner of the Pocking concentration camp was released from the hospital in Neuhaus, accompanied by three fellow sufferers. . . . It was his intention to help provide strong moral support to as many fellow believers as possible, to give them strength through the values of their religion, and to prepare them for emigration. A Bible and other items for the service came from Munich. Rabbi Meisels himself dug them up at a Munich cemetery where other rabbis had hidden them, following an old Jewish habit practiced during the earlier eras of persecution. The American military government and the district administrator of Griesbach supported the endeavors of the continually growing Jewish group in every way possible; they soon found themselves to be the owners of a provisional prayer house, to which was added, in August 1945, the ownership of a plot of land located on Tettenweiser Strasse, number 6.

The property had belonged to the former "brown" mayor, but was confiscated by the Americans and later made available to the Jewish community. According to an article in the Rottal regional edition of the *PNP* from 26 September 1947, "A program of action was devised almost immediately and today it can be considered as having reached its aims. A rabbinical position was established and regular instruction in economics and cultural studies was introduced."

According to Friedrich Appel, who was quoted in the 22 November 1990 issue of the *PNP* in an article with the headline "FABRICATION AND TRUTH," "About 10,000 Hungarian Jews" were living in the Waldstadt camp by September 1945. This figure is probably exaggerated, as documents from the UNRRA speak of 7,380 people, regardless of the fact that only a fraction of whom were from Hungary. Many of them were likely

former concentration camp prisoners from various countries. In January
1947 the Jewish Committee was elected in the presence of Herr Frühling,
the director of the UNRRA. Rabbi Meisels was chosen, with fifty out of
eighty-two votes, as the new chairman of the Pocking Jewish community.
In order to guarantee the internal structure, an honorary court consisting
of six people was also elected. Georg Osterholzer, who at the time was
community and district councilman, said in a 25 May 1992 interview:

> This was a problem for us. Kirchham only had about one hundred
> inhabitants. All of a sudden there were 1,000 barracks in the camp, filled
> with strangers. The Jews had their own commune there; they had noth-
> ing to do with us. The UNRRA made sure they were all cared for. It
> went so far that the Americans threatened us that if we did not fulfill our
> delivery quotas [of livestock, eggs, grain, milk, etc., to the DP camp] our
> cattle would simply be taken out of the farmers' stables. We were a com-
> munity rich in cattle and so we always delivered the quota amount,
> more or less. On one occasion a calf was stolen and taken over to the
> Jewish camp. We were powerless to do anything against this. They
> wouldn't let the German police enter [the camp] back then.

There were more than enough problems—internal as well as external.
And the benevolence of the Germans was not exactly abundant. The
Pocking community administration in particular showed itself to be dis-
approving and suspicious of the Pocking Jewish community. The mayor
of Pocking, Herr Wenig, for instance, assigned a newly vacated apartment
to a former Wehrmacht colonel rather than to a Jewish refugee family
with small children. In another case Rabbi Meisels asked in vain to make
available two rooms in downtown Pocking to serve as classrooms for Jewish adolescents. Mayor Wenig simply informed him that he was under
no obligation to look for such accommodations, that the Jews should do
that for themselves. This resulted in a scandal: in an open letter Rabbi
Meisels accused the mayor of having refused the establishment of Jewish
businesses and trade facilities, stating as a reason that there already were
enough of them:

> You kept finding fresh excuses to turn down projects of the Jewish com-
> munity. . . . Don't you know that the Pocking Jewish community con-
> sists of former concentration camp prisoners from Pocking who have
> lost their good health, their existence, their families, and their posses-
> sions as a result of having been forced into slave labor by the Nazis? You
> are continuing to complicate the lives of these Jews, who have been so

severely affected by the Nuremberg race laws. Through these actions you are violating legal directives and are disregarding the orders issued by the state commission for people who have been persecuted for racial, political, and religious reasons. We do not care for your pretty words and promises, as none of them have been realized so far.

Neither did Rabbi Meisels show any understanding for the fact that Mayor Wenig had not assigned even one of the fifty available living spaces to the Jewish community, even though it was in dire need of at least two of them. The quarreling continued and daily life was arduous. With some major assistance from private initiatives, The *PNP* eventually came to acknowledge the tasks accomplished by the Jewish community. Entitled "THE MINIATURE STATE OF POCKING," an extensive retrospective account was published. The subtitle promised an engaging report: "THE WORK OF THE JEWISH COMMUNITY—REPARATIONS OF THE HEART." However, the article went on to state very openly that the community enjoyed a "mixed reputation." On one hand there was its excellent location as well as the neighboring prosperous industries. On the other hand, however, there was its role as the headquarters of the black market in Lower Bavaria; this was made possible thanks to an affluent agricultural industry and busy trade with foreigners; "evil tongues had long claimed a connection [of these phenomena] to the Jewish community." The article concluded thus:

> Here and there the seed of a racial hatred instigated by the Nazis became virulent. But anyone who has followed the development of the small Jewish community from its most humble beginnings . . . will be surprised about the cleanliness and the enthusiastic work ethic evident in this "small state within a state." It is thanks to the Jewish initiative that Pocking has obtained its own theater company and achieved a high cultural standard. Leisure activities in Pocking are now served by the DP café, a reading room, and sports facilities. The desire for productive work was instilled and developed. Its own search committee succeeded in bringing together various families. Of the 117 members in the Jewish community living in downtown Pocking more than half of them are employed. Five of them own businesses or hold equivalent licenses.

At the time, seven members of the Jewish community were mechanics, twelve worked as tailors, nine were agricultural workers, five were carpenters, six were locksmiths, and four were shoemakers: the Jewish community had teachers, merchants, public servants, and one nurse. The community kitchen was "operating well." Eighteen persons were employed by the city of Pocking. The Jewish community had even established a dental technicians' school at the Pocking-Waldstadt camp. It was managed by a German dentist and financially supported by the Bavarian State Commissioner Dr. Philipp Auerbach. As early as the fall of 1947 five students were being educated and trained there. The engine factory in the neighboring town of Sulzbach had started to train several Jewish DPs as mechanics. Language courses in English as well as in Hebrew could be taken up directly at the Pocking-Waldstadt camp. A rather interesting book cataloguing an exhibit that ran from 25 October 1988 to 22 January 1989 at the Germanisches Nationalmuseum in Nuremberg and titled *Siehe, der Stein schreit aus der Mauer—Geschichte und Kultur der Juden in Bayern* (Observe, the stone screams forth from within the wall—the history and culture of the Jews in Bavaria) reveals what was not to be found in the *PNP:*

> The Jewish DP camp in Pocking, which was under the direct supervision of the 3rd district in Regensburg and administered by the UNRRA, or the IRO Passau, respectively, was one of the largest of its kind with 8,000 occupants. A fairly large group of orthodox Chabad-Hassidim Jews congregated there. As a result the only Lubavitz Yeshiva-Tomchei Tmimmim in the U.S.-occupied zone, which understood itself as a successor of the Yeshiva founded in Lubavitz in the year 1897, was established in Pocking. The more than two hundred pupils of the Pocking Yeshiva, which was provided with Yiddish and Hebrew literature as well as with religious texts by the AJDC [American Jewish Distribution Committee], were introduced by eight teachers to the traditional teachings of the Chabad-Hassidim, whose teachings center around spiritual joy. In addition to the Yeshiva, the Pocking camp had a Talmud-Torah, a Yawne, and an orthodox girls' school, as well as an orthodox Kibbutz. Pocking also had, along with the cities of Munich and Nuremberg, its own Schochtim class, where butchers were instructed in how to slaughter cattle according to Jewish kosher regulations.

At the time, many camp residents had intended to immigrate to Palestine. Yet many who received visas to the Netherlands, Canada, Argentina, or Belgium decided to go to there instead, in order to establish a secure existence as soon as possible. These countries were particularly interested in those who had worked in the timber and coal mining industries. Those who had remained in Pocking were instructed by Rabbi Meisels that the most important goal for the Jewish community was to work toward a positive coexistence with the German population. Material reparations were secondary to "reparations of the heart." And he was convinced that this aim was worth the great effort he put into reaching it.

On 12 April 1948, the graduation exam for dental technicians was held in Pocking. These Jewish apprentices proved themselves to be highly accomplished. Rabbi Meisels, who presented the diplomas, described in detail the problems that had to be solved just in order to create this school. Master dental technician Tendler from Nuremberg praised the diligence of the graduates, and the Association of Dental Technicians congratulated them in their "exemplary accomplishments." Six months later the *PNP* reported in its local Rottal edition that "craftsmen are being trained for Palestine." The statement hardly concealed the obvious hope that the existence of such a large Jewish community just outside the city limits should be short in duration. The readers were informed in detail about issues that had earlier only been rumored about: as of May 1946 one of the largest ORT technical colleges in the U.S.-occupied zone had been established in a spacious hangar located at the former Pocking airport. It was the goal of the local ORT association to "provide solid occupational training" to the Jewish émigrés to Palestine. This was where they were to establish their own enterprises and found an industry "in order to make the country as independent as possible." In the fall of 1948, eighteen classes received instruction in thirteen different subjects; the eldest student was fifty-three years old. Of the thirty instructors, five were Germans. Herr Tannenzapf was the director.

Meanwhile, smaller classrooms were built surrounding the former hangar: locksmiths, electricians, car mechanics, telegraphers, radio technicians, dental technicians, upholsterers, watchmakers, weavers, tailors, tanners, and seamstresses set up their workshops in that area. Excellent teaching materials were provided; some classes were instructed in double shifts. The class of dental technicians contained about twenty students. Also in demand were careers as postal clerks, train engineers, or radio operators. Under the guidance of a Jewish master seamstress, women's lingerie and gentleman's shirts were manufactured. All together approximately 450 students attended these classes for about a year each. The Passau chamber of commerce assisted in conducting the exams, and diplomas were issued by the International Relief Organization (IRO) and the ORT. The final examination was nearly equivalent to the German apprentice exam. Afterwards many graduates went on to work for German companies, while others emigrated. The latter group consisted mostly of people between seventeen and twenty-five years of age. According to their testimonies, after their arrival in Palestine many of them served in the army.

Prejudice against the Jewish Community: Dog Meat and Superstition

In October 1947 the Jewish DP camp in Pocking-Waldstadt still was home to some 6,000 people. Josef Gaisberger, who then was a community employee in Pocking, still remembers to this day how a Jewish woman cried bitterly upon meeting his nephew for the first time. She had lost her own child, she told Gaisberger, and loved his nephew, spoiling him as though he was her own son. She wanted to see him every day, and gave him food and other small gifts that amounted to a small fortune in those times. Yet experiences such as these were almost never publicly acknowledged. Similarly, the press almost exclusively reported about incidents in which someone from the camp supposedly committed some kind of crime. Even though such things happened only rarely, and even more rarely resulted in any kind of injury to anybody, prejudices dominated the perception of the Pocking Jewish community for many years. The German population assumed an adversarial and suspicious attitude towards the community and overwhelming anti-Semitic prejudices tended to exaggerate cases of petty theft, for instance, into proportions suited for capital crimes. Under the heading "FRAUD WITH WHEAT FLOUR," for example, one could read in the *PNP* how an "inmate" of the Pocking camp and three DPs from Wetzlar (former concentration camp prisoners) were to be sentenced to one year imprisonment unless they emigrated to Poland or voluntarily joined a transport to Palestine. Sentenced DPs had to serve their prison time, as did all displaced persons, in Würzburg.

The *PNP* reported on another case: "In December 1946, Joseph Friedmann, the cook of the Jewish community, asked to have two cows slaughtered by the butcher August Eigner, as ordered by the chief of food supply, Herr Badasch, in order to meet the demand for additional meat for Christmas." Friedmann was sentenced to a penalty of five hundred reichsmarks for conspiracy to butcher on the black-market. The German butcher, on the other hand, did not receive any sentence. Shortly thereafter the *PNP* complained: "Outside the gates of the DP camp: Local police are powerless." Through such reporting the *PNP* helped reenforce public suspicion that members of the DP community were involved in numerous incidents of theft and black-market activity. It was claimed that the Pocking-Waldstadt DP camp was involved in the illegal transport of six to eight cattle per week, and that 1,100 cubic meters of wood had been stolen. IRO vehicles and several hundred bicycles were found in the camp, "most of which were stolen." German police could not get involved, it was said, because "the local military government for DP members issued bicycle permits without checking where the bicycles had been acquired." The fact that many locals delivered the cattle and bartered for the bikes in exchange for money, clothing, and food from the DPs was not mentioned.

Those local farmers who bartered for these goods still insist today that "the prices were fair," and that they had offered these goods to the DPs in hopes of receiving in exchange items that they could not have afforded anywhere else. As Georg Osterholzer stated in an interview of 22 May 1992:

> The trade there was very well organized, there was nothing corrupt about it. From radios to chocolate. They received packages from the Americans, from relatives, and from the government. They had things we could buy only years later. But they did not have bicycles, meat, and eggs. This is where we came in. It was a good deal for everyone involved. Nobody had enough of anything in those days, including them. They had to save up for a bike like that and so we gave them our bikes and our cattle in exchange for coal and sugar. Times were hard for everyone. We all had to stick together, otherwise many of us would have died. And many people did die in those days. Even children, especially the smaller ones. There was no way around it. We were just glad to have survived one more week.

When in February 1948 a fire at the barracks destroyed the camp synagogue and the school, the Passau fire brigade was called in vain. The *PNP* did not report on the fire in connection with the camp; instead their reports about the "rotten eggs," or about "dog meat and superstition" that were to be found in the camp became even more detailed. Public opinion against the Pocking Jewish community was manipulated to be increasingly negative: during an election meeting of the CSU in Pocking, the Bavarian Secretary of Justice Dr. Josef Müller allegedly addressed only those problems that the DPs had apparently brought upon the local population. It was reported with palpable disdain that "the association of black- and gray-market traders (within the camp)" was said to "have claimed in a resolution to the state government that its activities were somehow politically important for regional issues of sustenance," as entered into the

Bavarian Registry of Associations under file number 65. The activities of the association were documented in quite some detail, even mentioning the fact that "a declaration of suspicion had been made" against the Bavarian state government, because it had "created an atmosphere of panic that had compelled the public to make unwise acquisitions on the basis of false statistics." The article's ironic tone no doubt amused some of the readers, when it reported that "those colleagues [of black-market traders] who up to this point have refrained from joining the local trade association . . . are requested to henceforth refile any applications at the municipal office in Pocking." It became evident that no stone was left unturned in their attempts to discredit the activities within the camp. It was claimed again and again that the people in the "Jew camps" were economically much better off than the rest of the population.

In December 1948 it was reported that "26,000 American cigarettes were confiscated." In another case a motorist on his way from Waldstadt to Pocking allegedly attempted to escape a traffic control, yet his flight ended at a garden fence. The driver was arrested. A total of 179 chocolate bars were confiscated. The passers-by took whatever they could get their hands on, but most of it was allegedly later retrieved by the police. There seems to have been only one truly serious offense: under the pretense of providing a job for a twenty-one-year-old woman, one DP lured her into the camp, raped her, and locked her into a room. She finally was able to escape the next day.

The Dissolution of the Camp: A Handshake as Goodbye

Alois Wenig, the mayor of Pocking in 1947, had the following declaration published in February 1947: "With the exception of those from the Waldstadt camp, 105 Jews are registered today in the community of Pocking. I cannot imagine that the community of Pocking alone is in any way responsible for reimbursing them for crimes against Jews that they did not commit. I am not an anti-Semite . . . but neither am I a philo-Semite." And he shamelessly added: "Why do they want to stay in Pocking, of all places, anyway?"

In December 1947 the following headline appeared in the *PNP*: "ENGLISH PULLING OUT OF PALESTINE. INTEGRATION OF THE NEW JEWISH STATE INTO THE BRITISH EMPIRE IS PLANNED." As early as April 1948, the article reported, an new wave of emigration to Palestine was planned, "for which about ninety percent of the [Pocking-Waldstadt] camp population was expected to sign up." But when January 1948 arrived, only one Ukrainian man, three Poles, and one Hungarian decided to go "home." Initially everybody had to turn to the respective department of the administrative district of Passau, then to the department in Amberg. Only DPs who had married German women were "prevented from going abroad." "For the moment," the article continued, "Germans are not allowed to emigrate. Only healthy, young people between the ages of eighteen and thirty-five, and in special cases up to forty years of age" were accepted.

Two months later the *PNP* reported about new emigration possibilities for DPs, including, for instance, the offer that transit and meals would be paid for by the IRO and that a baggage allowance of up to one hundred kilograms would be free of charge. Before immigration could take place, however, clearance would have to obtained from the CIC, the criminal police, and the department of health, and intelligence tests were also conducted on those desirous of leaving. Of the 523 people who lived at the Maierhof camp in Passau, more than fifty percent immediately signed up for emigration; moreover, thirty percent of those from both the Danube camp (out of a total of 407 persons) and the Innstadt camp (out of a total of one hundred persons) signed up as well; ten percent of the camp in Pocking, which at the time still held a total of 5,469 persons, signed up.

On 27 October 1948, the *PNP* reported about yet another transport from the Waldstadt camp: one hundred Jewish families, "exclusively members of the tailoring industry," were leaving for Canada. The Waldstadt camp was set to be "evacuated for good" by 31 January 1949. Posters were going to be displayed announcing the event. The *PNP* reported that demonstrations and hunger strikes had been called within the camp in the event that the camp was to be evacuated by force. The general exodus continued: Julius Schneider, the chairman of the Jewish Committee in Eggenfelden officially announced that from the local district about 350 of the 800 Jews had emigrated between 1945 and 1947; another 150 had followed in December 1948; most of them emigrated to Palestine. In January 1949 an estimated fifty persons left, by February another 150, and by May 1949 the remaining one hundred persons had emigrated. Approximately three-fourths of these Jews went to Israel.

Just Pocking-Waldstadt seemed to be "stuck" with the many Jewish DPs. On 21 January 1949, one could read in the *PNP* that the transports leaving Pocking-Waldstadt had been "temporarily cancelled." Only a few craftsmen and their families were permitted to leave for Canada. One also could read that an empty barracks was dismantled and converted into firewood. Under the headline: "THE LAST DAYS OF WALDSTADT," an article appeared that stated: "Suppliers [of the camp] see their profits dwindle, the 'armada of negotiators' is leaving, the 'inmates' are selling everything that is 'not bolted to the ground,' including the windows of several dismantled barracks." It also was not kept secret that now there were more Germans than DPs living in the camp—in particular merchants who were hoping to make some easy money. Although all access roads were guarded by police, certain materials such as wood, coal, shoes, cocoa, and tea were still being traded in the camp. Allegedly wardrobes for storing clothes were being made into transport containers for the emigrants, and the forest had been ravished leaving only tree stumps, lime, and mud. At the end of January the military began standing guard outside the camp in order to prevent smuggling deals from being conducted. "Long rows of freight cars were standing ready at the loading ramp for those departing." Obviously many readers felt a sense of satisfaction to read that "the camp is emptying out." The Jews who left for the United States were initially taken to camps in the Bavarian cities of Ulm, Rosenheim, and Deggendorf. People leaving for Palestine were brought to the French city of Marseille, and travelers to Canada were sent to the Northern German city of Bremen.

On the night of 1 February 1949 five hundred Jews from Pocking-Waldstadt began their trip to Heidenheim and Schwäbisch Hall, while the patients at the camp hospital were transferred to Passau. The camp itself still held approximately five hundred people whose "imminent emigration to Palestine" rendered the need for them to be accommodated at a transit camp unnecessary. After the recognition of the State of Israel by Great Britain, when Jews interned on Cyprus were allowed to immigrate into Israel, the *PNP* even published a photograph of the occasion. At about the same time another fire broke out in the Waldstadt camp: one evening at about 9:30 P.M., a residential barracks that once served as the post office at Pocking II had caught fire, most likely due to an overheated oven. The *PNP* reported that its last residents were three families who had already packed up all their belongings and who had lost everything in the fire. The alcohol distillery, housed at the barracks, was destroyed as well. The *PNP* explicitly denied that arson may have been involved.

On the same page one could read the following headline: "EVACUATION, STEP BY STEP." Within the next few days the so-called small camp of Waldstadt would be "entirely vacated by the foreigners," because the chairman of the Neubürgerbund (new citizen's alliance) and president of the emergency parliament, Günter Goetzendorff, was currently in Munich discussing the future usage of the camp. The plans were already worked out in detail, and they had been forwarded to the state secretary for refugee affairs in Munich and the district planning commission in Regensburg. The consensus was that there existed an "eminent interest" in a project combining state and private enterprises on the camp grounds. The state was to undersign for a loan in the amount of two million deutschmarks, in the form of cooperative shares, and to remit it in advance in order to ame-liorate the "catastrophic housing emergency" that apparently existed in the area and made this project necessary. In doing so, however, the state man-aged to evade paying out unemployment and welfare money.

There was open competition for the "inheritance of the nearby air base." On 11 February 1949 the third item on the schedule of the Pock-ing community meeting outlined a plan to establish a vocational school on the former grounds of the camp; at least five hundred apprentices were expected to enroll. The main argument, however, was that the old air base would be ideal for a settlement of "crisis-proof small industries." Several relatively undamaged buildings were still standing, there was a connection to the railway tracks as well as access to water and power supplies, in addi-tion to a canal system. However, the IRO most likely would initially be returning the terrain to the U.S. Army. It might be years by the time the land would be back in the hands of the government planning commission. Therefore steps would have to be taken now. In the meantime the *PNP* reported with concern about the "the final days of the Pocking DP camp. Everything from the water pump to the last window pane is being disman-tled."

On the night of 14 February, the remaining five hundred DPs left the barracks for Marseille, via Munich. At the end of February the camp was to be handed over to the U.S. Army. "The evacuation of the camp con-cludes a significant chapter of postwar history for this country. The ad-ministrative district and its population now hope that the road is cleared for realizing the project of settlement and industrialization." The *PNP* also pointed out, however, "that some people were already getting burned." "Many people have their own ideas about what will remain in the Wald-stadt camp and who will inherit the pitiful remnants. Because most of it is now owned by the IRO or the U.S. Army, one often has to ask whether whoever acquires it should be considered at worst a thief and at best a receiver of stolen goods."

A week later one could read: "Waldstadt camp waiting to be handed over." The IRO commissioner von Dyk informed German authorities that the jurisdiction of the 3rd U.S. Army in Heidelberg was still valid and that therefore the surrender of the camp would have to be postponed by several days. Residents had been hoping that after this point two hundred apartments would begin to be built there, some in the form of row houses, others as single-family homes. There was a plan to separate the tracts of land into an industrial and business district, and a residential area on the other. The rest of the camp grounds could be reforested; it could be turned into a whole "garden city." At this point the emigration of Jewish DPs was coming to an close in the entire region.

The *PNP* also reported: "ISRAELITES ARE MOVING AWAY—AND MOVING IN." "Large groups" of Jewish DPs have also been leaving Eggenfelden in recent days. In the meantime, however, about six hundred new Jews had arrived from Pocking and Berlin, some two hundred of them illegally. In August 1949, 1,328 Jews still lived in Eggenfelden (570 lived in the camps, 758 outside the camps); exactly 264 people emigrated in November 1949, another 270 in January 1950 and 200 more later on. They, however, were never officially registered.

The lampoon of the *Passauer Neue Presse*, the *Passauer Grosse Fresse*, or "Passau Loudmouth," joked in early May on page one that an unforgettable sendoff had been arranged for the last DP: the church choir had performed the song *"Muss I denn, muss I denn zum Städtele hinaus,"* a rough translation of which would be "Do I, oh do I, have to leave town?" A record player could also be heard playing the song: *"Zum Abschied reich' ich dir die Hände,"* or "A handshake as goodbye." With this musical accompaniment, the volunteer fire brigade provided the mock funeral procession as the last of the DPs left Pocking-Waldstadt for their final resting place. The municipal administration now hoped that the premises, which had been occupied up to then, would be at their disposal within the next two or three years.

Pocking-Waldstadt: The Dream of a New German Settlement

On 15 March 1949, the IRO officially handed the camp over to the community of Pocking. In order to prevent looting there was a strong police presence, which included three patrol cars and thirty German civilian guards who were on duty around the clock, leading up until the time of transfer. The camp in Pocking-Waldstadt was to be transformed into "a new city in the Rott River valley." The area under consideration included ninety barracks, several large hangars, and close to two hundred hectares of land for developing. But after the last Jews had left the camp more than two thousand expellees began to arrive in Pocking-Waldstadt over time: there were Batschka-Germans as well as people from the Banat region of Hungary, previously settled by Germans, and from Silesia.

On 26 March 1949 a major rally took place in Pocking. Over two thousand people showed up and Dr. Wiederholz, a member of the county parliament, argued against establishing a new refugee camp for the new arrivals as the repair of the barracks alone would cost one million deutschmarks. With one of the hangars intact, they could potentially be turned into a sports field and an exhibition center, he argued, and some space had to be made available for recreational gardeners and a municipal forest. It was conceivable that 1,400 apartments could be built, which would accommodate close to 8,000 people. One hundred hectares of land would be reserved for construction projects, including schools and a hospital. The necessary investment sum was estimated to amount to fourteen million deutschmarks. The planning committee for this new city in Rottal hoped to receive start-up capital from the city of Pocking in the amount of approximately two million deutschmarks.

In May 1949 the statement was made that "construction work at the Waldstadt camp has begun." Yet, there was also some criticism: the barracks were in fact being only superficially repaired; the buildings were anything but solid; three to four hundred workers would be required for the project. When five hundred volunteers ultimately signed up, the *PNP* wrote: "Waldstadt camp creates flood of work for the government employment offices." The accommodations left behind by the Jewish DPs were now taken over by refugees of German origin. The ambitious plans of Pocking's citizens to build a new city on the area turned out to be unrealistic. Regarding the arrival of the refugees of German origin, people anxiously asked: "More foreigners in Waldstadt?" Hopes for "a real" settlement rose when at the end of June the Stuttgart-based chain company Eugen Braitsch arrived with some of their equipment and machines and set up an industry on the site. They began manufacturing bicycle and motorcycle chains and soon the company employed some four hundred workers. Only a few months later the company began plans to establish a second factory in Pocking-Waldstadt and to hire another three hundred workers. Still another branch would require fifty workers.

At the end of July the *PNP* reported on their "visit to the chain manu-facturing company Eugen Braitsch in the former Pocking air base." The company had leased two large halls at the air base. Originally they were actually producing grandfather clocks and supplied other companies. In Waldstadt the work spanned several shifts around the clock and soon workers were able to produce five thousand chains a day. There were plans to establish company-owned shops, where prices were up to twenty-five percent lower than anywhere else, and there was to be a cafeteria as well. The "plans for the Waldstadt camp" also indicated that only sixteen of the old barracks were to be taken down. The plans for settlement of the new refugees became more than dubious to the owners of the Rottalheim housing project, who planned to house many of these new arrivals.

Georg Osterholzer remembers the time when some of the barracks at the camp were dismantled and then rebuilt in the community of Pock-ing. "Initially they became part of the junior high school, which later on became the Pocking college-preparatory school." Yet in spite of all the efforts, nothing ever came of the plans for a real settlement: by the end of the 1950s the refugees had departed, as had the businesses from Pocking-Waldstadt. Shortly afterwards the German Armed Forces acquired this property, with its rich history. The place where concentration camp pris-oners had been tortured to death is today nothing more than a wheat field. In 1961 the German Bundeswehr, or the new Armed Forces of the Ger-man Federal Republic, took possession of the area and for the first time began to utilize the still existing barracks. Today almost nothing is left of them. Here and there a few remnants of a structure can be seen. "They were torn down in 1968/69," said troop commander Lieutenant Colonel Wunder, shortly before his discharge: "The neighbors are friendly. There are no problems, even though the tank battalions aren't exactly quiet." The airport runway, which as a part of their military strategy had never been officially fortified by the Nazis, was used in the 1950s as a starting and landing strip for private gliders. Two hangars were torn down soon afterwards. Only the concrete flooring on which they once stood still exists. The place that once was the old military stronghold of the Wehrma-cht now houses the clothing issuer of the Rottal Barracks of the German Armed Forces. A sign along the B 12 federal highway shows the way there; it is marked "ALTER HORST." In 1992 people became concerned that the

"Rottal Barracks" might be dissolved, as a central agency for the reception of asylum seekers was in the planning stages. And soon people in Pocking were anxiously asking yet again: "Foreigners, again, in Waldstadt?" The 23 December 1992 issue of the *Passauer Woche* newspaper published the following: "The mayor of Passau, Willy Schmöller, finally devised a way to get rid of the impending wave of asylum seekers, moving them from his barracks to the open land. The local district administrator, Hanns Dorfner, however, is fighting this initiative." When Konrad Kobler, a member of the state parliament, requested that eastern Lower Bavaria should not be completely "wiped out" in accommodating the asylum seekers, the *Passauer Woche* newspaper wrote: "Ten hand grenades for Chancellor [Helmut] Kohl. Whether betrayed or simply sold out, the region of Passau was at any rate made a fool of . . . by the decision to throw Kirchham onto the garbage pile." The conservative party, the CSU, was so desperately trying to hang on to its military bases that they even threatened the life of fellow conservative Chancellor Kohl for suggesting that the Kirchham base be closed.

The readers of the *Passauer Woche* also read that "the German Armed Forces always had been and always will be of major importance, and have been fully integrated into both the social and cultural climate of the region." The readers also were made aware of the fact, that "the member of the state parliament, Kobler, was hoping that the arguments were in fact hitting the Chancellor like hand grenades, that the sound of these powerful arguments would drone in his ears, and that the final announcement that the imminent breakup of the tank battalion . . . would ultimately be stopped by someone in Bonn putting his foot down." The protests by local politicians was so vehement that the people responsible in Bonn gave in and ordered the barracks to remain standing the way they were.

Abraham Eiboszyc—Five Deutschmarks Per Day Spent in the Concentration Camp

One of the few Jews who remained in eastern Bavaria originated from Poland and had arrived in Waldstadt in 1945 along with four hundred other prisoners. They had marched there on foot and had been trying to establish some kind of an existence. The parents of Abraham Eiboszyc were merchants. During the war they were deported by the Nazis. It is not known where they finally died. Abraham was married to his wife Lola in 1938. His wife and their four-year-old son were murdered in the gas chambers of Auschwitz. Abraham himself was imprisoned in various concentration camps and forced-labor commandos over a span of five and a half years.

In 1950 he settled in Passau and remarried; his wife was a Catholic. Every Christmas there would be a Christmas tree in his living room, his wife was very active in church, and his son was baptized as a Catholic. "There were no Jewish women to be had," he said. Until his death in 1985 Abraham was a member of the Straubing Jewish community. He attended services there for twenty-five years. He subscribed to Jewish newspapers and kept in touch with fellow Jews living in Munich and Straubing. But at age eighty, and after fifteen different operations, he was ill and weak and barely able to leave his house during these his final years.

Abraham had come to terms with his life in the Diaspora. He accepted his Christian environment and neither wanted to encounter problems because he was a Jew, nor did he want to cause any. It was his wish that his son would have a secure and solid place in society. He enabled him to have the best education possible and even built a house that the son would later inherit. He was proud of his son and had him baptized to avoid any possible difficulties of integration. In one of his many calendars Abraham noted both the Jewish as well as the Christian holidays.

For many years he celebrated the high Jewish holidays at the residence of Rabbi Salzberg in Passau, even though he believed Salzberg to be a parasite. He kept in close touch with Flora Salzberg, "who knew how to live life." Twice he received visits by former Jewish concentration camp prisoners who had been "with him, back then, in Pocking-Waldstadt." He would have liked to live "as a Jew," following the dictates of the religion. "But how would that have been possible?" he wondered continuously. When I once asked him if he had ever thought of moving to Straubing or Munich he told me that he had actually once rented a room in Straubing. But then he had fallen ill. "I have neuralgic pain that survives from those times that have been forgotten only on the surface." Without money he never dared to begin again in Munich or Straubing; he could never have afforded to buy a house with such little money, especially not in Munich. "And whenever I had more money I always got sick. I had to spend everything on doctors and stay in my sickbed; others were able to work and earn money. But the doctors helped me; what wouldn't you give to be free of pain? You would give everything. What is money when you're in constant pain?" By the time he was old he had become too accustomed to his environment to want to move again.

However he sometimes still played cards or visited acquaintances and friends. Abraham became a successful and respected businessman. Right up to the end he lived according to the motto: "Arguing is pointless—it leads to nothing—better to turn a blind eye!" He turned a blind eye himself once, when he was told by a German: "They forgot about you when they were gassing people!" He did not want to quarrel or fight, he avoided conflict. A week later, he told me, the person who said this was sorry. Abraham did receive reparations: five deutschmarks for each day he had to spend in a concentration camp. But the money was nearly all spent. "There were witnesses to be paid, the notary, and the lawyer—a Jew, by the way, from Munich. After all the fees there was nothing left over—all I could buy with the remaining money was an old hat!" Later he received a small additional payment for health damages resulting from the long years he had to endure imprisoned in concentration camps. In the final years of his life he was "just glad to be able to walk." Up to the end he kept an article from the *Süddeutsche Zeitung* written in 1958 in one of his drawers. The article was titled: "EVEN THE PERSECUTORS ARE RECEIVING REPARATIONS."

Up until 1985 he did not tell anyone what he had once suffered through; neither the public prosecutors who were searching for witnesses, nor journalists who wanted to report about it got to hear his story. "It's too late," he said, "they should have done this forty years ago. What good is it to bring old men to justice?" He looked at me for a long time and added: "Forty years ago I had better nerves." He wanted peace, but he could not forget the past. He wanted to live as well as he could manage. Abraham Eiboszyc is the only member of his family to have survived the Holocaust.

Maintaining the Graves

Nothing is left today of the mass graves at the Pocking train station. Mayor Jakob states that "the exact location of the mass grave at the station is unfortunately not known any longer." Former mayor Franz Krah even claims to "never have heard about [the graves]." But Bruno Müller and Josef Gaisberger, both long-standing citizens of Pocking, remember exactly where the former mass grave was located: approximately one hundred meters north of the train station itself, between the railroad embankment and the slope right next to the old soccer field.

Through an ordinance issued on 22 June 1957 by the Bavarian Ministry of Finance, maintenance of the cemeteries where victims of National

Socialist persecution lay was transferred to the Bavarian Castles, Parks, and Lakes Administration. The "constant obligation to maintain the memorials and memorial sites of the victims of deportation" derives from a bulletin published on 22 April 1945, regarding the 23 October 1954 agreement between the Federal Republic of Germany and the Republic of France. In 1957, within the framework of this treaty, the French search committee for war victims transported eleven corpses from the Pocking-Waldstadt concentration camp to their respective countries of birth and transferred the bodies of eighty-five unknown persons to the concentration camp memorial cemetery in Flossenbürg. They lie there today, in field C, rows 6b and 7b, bearing the grave numbers 1756 to 1840. The fifty-six bodies that were exhumed at the Pocking train station lie in the same field, in rows 7b to 8a, bearing the grave numbers 1841 to 1896. Allegedly there are no bodies left at the memorial site next to the federal highway B 12. This means that more than one hundred corpses must have somehow secretly disappeared—an explanation that hardly seems credible.

The costs for the care and maintenance of the memorial site in Pocking vary according to the extent of efforts made for its upkeep. The administrative office responsible for this task informed me that "in the early 1980s an extensive renovation of the memorial site was undertaken," and that "the effort resulted in costs of 40,000 deutschmarks. In 1984 the gravel paths had to be resurfaced and renovated at a cost of 10,000 deutschmarks, and that in 1989 other repairs to the surrounding walls were made at a cost of 6,500 deutschmarks. The costs for continual upkeep at the present time amount to approximately 2,200 deutschmarks per year." "The removal of graffiti and other damages is being remunerated by State funds." In spite of written inquiries the agency refused to share information about whether this kind of removal is actually taking place and if so, how often. The criminal investigation department and the district attorney's office of Passau proved to be a bit more communicative on the subject. . . . A brief look into file number 2 VJs3131/91 was sufficient to prove, for example, that a desecration had occurred in 1991: at that point a man by the name of Alfons Auer had filed a report that the metal sign at the federal highway B 12 pointing out the memorial site had been completely destroyed. During that night right-wing extremists had also torn up the cast iron sprinkler system and carved a huge swastika approximately fifteen feet tall, as well as two SS symbols measuring over six feet each, into the gravel paths. The perpetrators were never identified.

There is also no information contained in the files concerning "the exact content of the aforementioned inscriptions." Documents in the possession of Lipot Yehuda Meisels prove that the recollections of eyewitnesses are reliable: the empty stone tablet next to the B 12 federal highway had displayed the names of companies who had assisted in building the memorial site.

The three stone tablets at the base of the obelisk outlined in six languages the history of the concentration subcamp. Furthermore, each of the three large empty stone tablets to the right and left sides of the obelisk mentioned the names of all the ninety-six people who were known to have been killed at the concentration camp, including their dates of death. The final line commemorated the unidentified dead who were buried in the vicinity. Allegedly, the engraved, tar-colored inscription was "weather-beaten as early as the year 1958. A restoration was not planned." The Federal Republic of Germany has thus accomplished what the National Socialists were not able to: the latter killed the victims but the Federal Republic has robbed them of their identity even in their death by taking away their names. Strangely enough it was the office legally in charge of preservation of the memorial, the Bavarian Castles, Parks, and Lakes Administration, which had all inscriptions, names, and dates of death removed. This was not the act of a neo-Nazi; it was an order from the State. The agency responsible for this is, as it was then, the Ministry of Finance.

At the time, Fritz Schäffer, the uncle of Passau's historic conservator, was minister of finance. It is sufficient to take one look at Dr. Lily Gardner Feldman's essay "The Special Relationship between West Germany and Israel" to realize that the entire issue is even more embarrassing: on 30 September 1945 Fritz Schäffer was dismissed as Bavarian prime minister by the Americans. He also was the one who resisted, until the very end, any restitution agreements with the State of Israel. Schäffer would have been one hundred years old in 1988. An exhibit was held, and a matching catalogue was published, during that period to honor Schäffer so that his name would not be forgotten. Passau not only named a large riverside promenade after this man, they also established a memorial in his honor.

Other Graves

Just behind the memorial site at the B 12 federal highway, the dead bodies of forty-five Jewish children and three adults are buried, all of whom had been held at the DP camp. When in 1948 the district administration office made an inquiry at the building supervisory board of the county asking about the situation of the Jewish cemeteries, it was informed on 2 July:

> Chief Rabbi Meisels came to the conclusion that a plaster plaque, which in his estimation served as a provisional plaque, listing the German firms that had participated in erecting the memorial had been partially removed and smashed. The plaster plaque itself was not found at the memorial itself but instead behind the entrance steps of the concentration camp memorial. In the opinion of Meisels, half of it had been destroyed by force, and the desecration of the memorial was in with his estimation related to this act. An on-site inspection determined that a one- to two-centimeter thick plaster plaque, which was not in itself very sturdy and only superficially held on to the plaster foundation through a layer of fabric, had fallen off as a result of environmental conditions.

Behind the concentration camp memorial, adjacent to the embankment, a cemetery for Jewish children was built. The enclosure of the children's cemetery consisted of an area enclosed by about four to six posts connected by wire. The wire as well as the posts had been removed; the holes where the posts had been were still clearly visible. Rabbi Meisels interpreted the missing wire as connected to the desecration of the concentration camp memorial and the cemetery. The conclusion by the (non-Jewish) men on site, however, was the following:

> For a person not familiar with the area, the enclosure described above does not indicate the existence of a cemetery. Crosses or other similar symbols or inscriptions do not mark the graves. The graves themselves are recognizable, depending on age of the grave mounts, with elevations measuring fifteen centimeters in height, forty centimeters in length, and eighty centimeters in width, with an approximate distance of eighty centimeters from each other. There are no plants, etc., to mark them. There also is no sign indicating the existence of the graves. It is very conceivable that someone who happened to pass by and was in need of some wire, which is still rationed, might have stolen it, and the posts along with it.

The district attorney's office categorically refused to make any further inquiries. On 30 September it was added that these were graves of dead children whose parents had lived at the Waldstadt camp and not able to afford a transfer to the closest Jewish cemetery. One fresh mound was marked with a wooden plank without any inscription, another with a Star of David made from cardboard, with an inscription. It was suggested that the burial ground be established as a cemetery or to have the corpses transferred to the closest Jewish cemetery. On 23 July 1948 the county police of Griesbach informed the headquarters of Lower Bavaria/Upper Palatinate that the concentration camp cemetery opposite the train station measured twenty-four meters in length and was surrounded by a wooden picket fence of about 1.6 meters in height. The posts were made of stone; two boards were missing and one post was defective. It was marked by a wooden cross that measured four meters in height, and two wooden Stars of David, each three meters in height. While the cross was mounted on a concrete base, the Stars of David were loosely anchored in the ground.

On 20 December 1948, another local inspection took place. Chief Rabbi Meisels, the head of the local building office, and the chief of the district inspection office of the county police determined that since 29 September seven graves had been added at the children's cemetery. At the time the Jewish community was planning to fence in the cemetery: five wall posts would be erected on an area measuring fifty meters in width, between which a hedge was to be planted at a later time. A fox's den that had existed between the embankment of the memorial and the cemetery since October was left untouched. The broken plaster plaque meanwhile had been replaced by a stone tablet.

Half a year later the last DPs were forced to leave, and the Jewish community dissolved. It is not clear whether plans for the cemetery were ever approved: the community of Pocking no longer has any documents relating to the matter. It is certain, however, that a short time later the community sold the area for a small sum to the farmer Ludwig Auer. He converted it into a grain field. Auer, who owns the farmland behind the Pocking memorial, talked openly about the forgotten children's graves. "Nobody ever cared about them," he says. These graves were never included in the planning of the memorial site nor were they taken over by the state administration, because they were not officially considered as falling under the category of those graves "of victims of war and regimes of terror" that the state was legally obligated to maintain. As if these children were not too weak to survive as a result of their mothers being liberated from the concentration camp while sick and suffering from malnutrition. As if they had not died because roots and moss were not suitable baby food. As if the parents who had to bury their infants would not interpret their death as the result of a regime of terror.

According to a resolution from 11 January 1952 information about registrations for grave sites of Jewish cemeteries up to that date had to be added to the existing documents. On 6 February 1952 district administrator Dr. Wimmer received the so-called B List to the Pocking community administration, into which information about the concentration camp cemetery as well as the mass grave at the train station had to be entered. Because future maintenance of the graves depended on these entries, it was requested that the authorities "submit reliable information by 18 February."

On 14 February the mayor of Pocking informed the district administration of Griesbach that only two graves existed, both of which were "in excellent condition"; a statement that was later modified by the district administrator in a letter to the government changing the classification of their condition from "excellent" to "good." The mayor listed "ninety-eight dead" for the memorial at the B 12 federal highway, a number that the county administrator did not consider accurate even then; this number was based solely on those identifiable names still listed on the six stone tablets, and completely ignored the many unidentified victims. The mayor stated, that "merely a large cross and two boards reminding of the dead" had been erected at the station, a fact that was not even mentioned in the official report. On the final day, 18 February, Dr. Wimmer reported to the government of Lower Bavaria "that no Jewish cemetery existed in the county of Griesbach," this despite the fact that the B List was completed.

According to an agreement between the State of Bavaria and the Regional Association of the Jewish Cultural Community of Bavaria, the abandoned cemeteries were to be maintained in the future by the latter organization. However, the cooperation of individuals was absolutely necessary; on page 705, section 1, of issue number 37 of the ministerial bulletin *MABI* from 27 September 1957, it is specified that only those individuals who consider the utilization of the grassy area of the cemetery important or who "are in need of additional income," were listed as "suitable." The article continued, reporting that "the maintenance . . . generally includes the upkeep of the cemetery enclosure and the cemetery paths, as well as regular cutting of the grass, removal of weeds, and the repair of toppled gravestones." Further points followed:

2.   The transfer of maintenance duties . . . does not preclude the fact that local communities and police will keep a watchful eye for the purposes of safekeeping and preservation of these locations. . . .

Willful damage, removal of gravestones, etc., . . . are to be communicated to the regional association. As a preventive measure to protect abandoned Jewish cemeteries, local communities are asked to have durable signs installed in clear view at the entrances to the cemeteries and bearing the following inscription: "THIS CEMETERY IS SUBJECT TO PROTECTION BY THE GENERAL PUBLIC. DAMAGE, DESTRUCTION AND ANY OTHER REPREHENSIBLE ACTIVITIES ARE PUNISHABLE BY LAW (ACCORDING TO ARTICLE 168, SECTION 304 OF THE STGB PENAL CODE)."

It also included the following addendum: "Any costs that result can be charged to the Regional Association of the Jewish Cultural Community."

Both the children's cemetery of Pocking and the mass grave at the train station have long since ceased to exist. All traces of their presence have quietly been removed. The Straubing Jewish community wants to buy the piece of farmland where the children lie buried and build a memorial. No plans ever existed for building a memorial for the Russians who were murdered at the Rottwerk, not far from the Pocking train station. The names of those concentration camp prisoners are as unknown today as is their fate. For the Hungarians who served with the German troops and the Hungarian SS, on the other hand, a special cemetery was built in Pocking by the German War Cemeteries Commission. It remains extremely well kept to this day. The names of the dead as well as their birth and death dates are listed individually, both engraved on the stones as well as inscribed on a large copper death register that is on public display. Except for the pompous formal opening ceremony in 1948, hardly any memorial ceremonies worth mentioning have taken place at the Pocking memorial. An exception was the year 1946, on the remembrance day for victims of Fascism, when former prisoners from the camps in Schlupfing and Pocking-Waldstadt laid down a wreath. In the year 1957, only the following information about former concentration camp prisoners was allegedly to be found at the community administration office in Pocking:

Lokoiec, Majer, born 1927 in Ciechanow/Poland, moved to USA in the year 1948.

Mandel, Dezsö, born 1926 in Kasche/USSR, moved to Amberg on 29 October 1949.

Niski, Heinrich, born 1924 in Kosice/USSR, moved to unknown location on 4 November 1949.

Pasternak, Otek, born 1914 in Msrezowow/Poland, moved to USA on 1 January 1950.

Perkal, Adam, born 1901 in Warsaw, moved to unknown location in
1947.

Reinstein, Abraham, born 1911 in Miechow/Poland, moved to Canada
in October 1948.

Ritter, Richard, born 1924 in Vienna, moved to New York on 21 October 1949.

Rosenfeld, Jendo, born 1925 in Hust/SCCR, allegedly the youngest
prisoner working in the kitchen at the Pocking-Waldstadt concentration camp.

There allegedly are only seven persons known by name, who were part of
the air base. They are:

Epple, Hans, scrap metal dealer
Große, Gerhard, merchant
Sarne, Hermann, merchant
Dohrmaier, Karl, civil servant
Franke, Johannes, former staff sergeant in Cologne-Wahn
Weiß, Karl, general practitioner
Scheier, Ignaz

The last air base commander allegedly was a colonel by the name of
Hörder. By the end of the war he supposedly lived in Passau and later
moved to his hometown, assumed to be Essen. The records of the Central
Agency of County Legal Administration in Ludwigsburg for the year 1967
register the following:

> The officials from the communities of Pocking and Kirchham who were
> in office at the end of the war have for the most part all died. However,
> former members of the air base still live close by. Some of them were
> questioned. They concurred not to have had any knowledge about what
> happened at the camp. Some of them did see the prisoners, however
> they claimed to have had no dealings with them. Records concerning
> registrations and discharges at the end of the war are no longer available
> at the Kirchham community administration. Neither Landgräber nor
> any other SS members in the Pocking community were still living. The
> name Landgräber is no longer known either to the former prisoners or
> to the former members of the air base. It is most likely that the guard
> personnel resided at the air base itself.

At about the same time, a wreath was laid down at the mass grave opposite the Pocking train station. Afterwards representatives of the political
parties and administrations as well as victims and many residents came

together at the Stadler Hall in Pocking. Following this event, Memory was relegated to the political sidelines; it was no longer desirable and became viewed as something negative. Soon afterwards, functions of this kind would come to be considered "communist agit-prop" (or agitation propaganda)—the effects of the cold war were beginning to be seen. It was not until 1985, forty years after the end of the war, that the German-Israeli Association in Pocking organized an hour of remembrance at the con-centration camp memorial. Since then an annual commemoration takes place in honor of the victims, even if few people attend it.

Cemetery without Graves

Lieutenant Colonel Wunder willingly gave me access to the site plans of the prison camp and the "Barracks City" of Waldstadt. He also gave me permission to photograph the now rudimentary structures from "back then." However, I was never given photographs of the old barracks. I was told by the troop administration clerk Herr Damm that "an entire battalion is standing in front of it, you can see almost nothing." Allegedly the community administration in Pocking does not possess either photographs or any other documents pertaining to the camp. Frau Dorfner, the wife of the current district administrator, had been employed as secretary at the community administration office in Kirchham during that time. She was helpful in referring me to other people and also recalls a card catalogue of war prisoners, but remembers almost nothing herself. The employees at today's Kirchham community offices claim to never have seen such documents.

In the official death registers from 1943 to 1945 only two dead infants belonging to "Eastern workers" are recorded; there are no records of con-centration camp prisoners. Newspaper editor Bernhard Brunner of the *PNP* published an article about the "cemetery without graves" in 1990, but did not name any of his sources. He claims that at the time certain documents pertaining to the issue had "fallen into his hands," but he did not remember when or from whom they had come. Nor does he remember what became of them. The district administration office claims no longer to have any documents. The mayor of Pocking, Herr Jakob, declared in 1991: "There are no known survivors." Unfortunately there also existed no formal archive, so that any further information that might have helped identify survivors or others was unavailable. At the time of this writing, however, the new curator for local history was in the process of establishing just such an archive.

In May 1992 it finally became official that "there are simply no records" pertaining to anything concerning the history of the camp and its prisoners. Albert Krah, who wrote his university thesis about the development of the city of Pocking, simply "omitted" those years from his study, as "no precise data were available." In November 1987 Albert Krah gave me access to two sworn statements by his predecessor Stephan Valentin Bühl and sent me a list of former Jewish concentration camp prisoners, which belonged to the Jewish Religious Committee. Today these documents are also considered to be "no longer available." Josefa Weishäupl from the town of Aicha vorm Wald claimed in a *PNP* article of 16 June 1993: "There never was a concentration camp in Pocking," and "there exists, however, a memorial there for executed Russian POWs." Ms. Weishäupl continues, complaining: "Why is Ms. Rosmus even granted access to the archives when it is clear that she will use it to sully the reputation of our city of Passau and its inhabitants? It is the moral duty of our acting mayor, the city councilmen, and the district administrator to take action against this kind of defamation." Even Katharina Titkemeyer, the daughter of a Passau physician, tried her hand at revisionist history. In her 9 May 1993 letter to the editor of the well-known *Jerusalem Post* she claimed that the inscriptions at the concentration camp memorial site were in fact never removed and that indeed the opposite was true: that the Bavarian state government had long since published all information claimed to have been "discovered" by Anna Rosmus. The editor of the *Jerusalem Post*, however, knew that these assertions did not correspond to the facts and refused to publish this falsification of history. After all, Rabbi Meisels was living in Jerusalem and was a particularly active member of this community. He held on to hundreds of documents, many of which he had shared with Yad Vashem. Holocaust denial is not so easy where there are survivors to prove otherwise.

And precisely for the reason that no exact information was available, the Pocking community council approved, in April 1993, a motion to build a museum that will display numerous, previously unpublished documents from private collections of the survivors of the camp. The present plans are to put a permanent exhibit there as well as to establish a traveling exhibit that will be taken to schools and other institutions. I continue to collect documents and to raise funds in order someday to make this dream a reality.